OFFICE
Communications

DARNLEY
PUBLICATIONS
INC.

Legal deposit – Bibliothèque et Archives nationales du Québec, 2007
Legal deposit – Library and Archives Canada, 2007

ISBN 978-2-923623-02-3

Printed in Canada

Catalog No.: TABC2

Author:
Ray E. Staszko

Editor-in-Chief:
Claude P. Major, Ph.D.

Project Manager:
Francine Hébert, M.Ed.

Contributing Editors:
Joanne Labre
Michael Boulay

Copy Editor:
Edward Cooney

Design and Layout:
Saskia Nieuwendijk
Michael Gonzalez

TABLE OF
Contents

TABLE OF
Contents

Chapter 4

INTRODUCTION

Among the many daily responsibilities of administrative assistants, handling office communications is surely one of the most dynamic. From managing incoming and outgoing communications to coordinating meetings and making travel arrangements, office professionals have direct involvement in a wide range of vital activities. This text will explore some of the most common communication duties of today's administrative assistants.

We will start by examining more closely the equipment and processes that are used in both electronic and paper-based forms of communication. With regard to paper documents, this text will concentrate on how to process and transmit them, rather than how to compose or generate them.

This text will describe some tasks that are performed using computers, however the emphasis will be more on the stages of the operations, rather than technical procedural steps (what on-screen buttons to select, etc.) That type of detail can only be provided in the context of studying a specific software package. The information we provide at this stage will be applicable to whatever software you may find yourself using in a given work situation. Once you are well grounded in the basic procedures, learning "which buttons to select" will be much easier, because you will have a greater understanding of exactly what you are doing and why.

Chapter 1

TELECOMMUNICATIONS
Equipment and Systems

Telephone Based Systems

Telephone communications systems have changed dramatically many times over the decades since the device was first invented by Alexander Graham Bell in the 1870s. A detailed history is unnecessary and impractical to this presentation. However, a brief look back at some older approaches that have come and gone (and in some cases returned) over the years may help provide a better understanding of modern systems.

For a long time it was not possible for a phone user to dial another party directly. Antique telephones had a mouthpiece, an earpiece, and a lever that was clicked to get the attention of an operator at a main switchboard. Every phone user was identified by a cord with a plug on it, and a corresponding socket, that was built into the control panel at the operator's console. When you told the operator to whom you wanted to place a call, the operator had to physically take the plug attached to your line and place it into the socket of the party you were trying to reach, then initiate a ring tone. As systems grew, calls got passed from operator to operator but the switching was still accomplished manually. No one placed a phone call without the assistance of an operator.

As you know, it eventually became possible for home telephone users to place calls, first locally and eventually long distance as well, by "dialing" directly. Electronic equipment did the switching and operators were no longer needed for that service. The term "dialing" came from the fact that for several decades phones had a rotary dial that was used to enter phone numbers. You stuck one finger in a hole in the dial that lay over the number you wished to select, rotated the dial until you reached a stop point, then released it and went on to the next digit in the number. It was quite an innovation when push button phones came along and replaced the old dials. Your parents probably still remember using them, and perhaps you remember seeing them growing up, depending on your age and where you live.

Oddly enough, when it came to corporate phone systems, the role of the switchboard operator lasted a lot longer than in residential service. The role is rapidly fading now, but has not entirely disappeared. Until fairly recently most calls placed to a business phone number were answered by a switchboard operator, perhaps stationed at the main reception desk. This person often did little but answer incoming calls, because in many cases all calls had to be answered at this location. The switchboard operator would greet the phone caller and determine to whom the caller wished or needed to be connected. It's been a long time since a switchboard operator had to physically pull a cord and plug it into a socket to transfer the call, but the basic principle remained the same. All incoming calls (and earlier all outgoing calls as well) had to be funneled through a single person or workstation.

Outgoing calls were liberated from this central stranglehold earlier than incoming calls. It became possible for someone using an individual line inside the office to get a dial tone and place a call without the assistance of the switchboard operator. However, for a long time incoming calls still had to be answered at the central station first and then transferred to a local extension.

We are describing this practice in past tense, but there are still many organizations that use switchboard operators to answer at least some of their incoming calls. The equipment has become more sophisticated. Instead of bulky headphones cabled to the work station, today's switchboard workers often have light-weight wireless earpieces and microphones that allow them greater comfort and freedom of movement. All call switching is electronic, and there are many special features that allow options for outgoing calls. The option of a central switchboard is often maintained in organizations that tend to receive a lot of calls from the general public, who don't necessarily know to whom they need to speak or what the extension number may be of a specific department or employee. Sometimes there is an option for callers to enter the extension number themselves when it is known and thereby bypass the switchboard operator, and for others to stay on the line and wait for the operator to assist them.

However, central switchboards create problems, and many organizations have moved away from them either partially or completely. One obvious problem is that if too many people try to call the organization at the same time, and most or all of them need to speak to the switchboard operator or operators, the system can easily become overloaded. Potential customers can be lost if they become frustrated with having to wait for their call to be answered. We have all experienced being put "on hold" by the system while we wait for "the next available operator" to take our call. A caller can end up waiting many minutes in order to have a very brief conversation with the switchboard operator to get their call transferred to the proper extension.

There are two main ways in which businesses have attempted to reduce this problem. One is by installing computerized answering systems. The call is first answered by a voice machine that presents the caller with a series of options. "Press 1 to place a service call. Press 2 to make an inquiry about your account. Press 3, etc." This system alleviates a large part of the bottleneck because the computer, unlike a human switchboard operator, can answer more than one call at the same time. Then

there may be a series of mini switchboards at the various general destinations. For example, one mini switchboard may handle service calls, another account inquires, etc. Sometimes this second layer is handled by a live person, but in other cases after the call is directed for the first time, there is a second level of computerized answering and questioning to get the client's needs focused more specifically. In organizations that handle a large volume of incoming calls and don't unnecessarily want to speak to all callers personally, sometimes the caller never does reach a human being. An attempt is made to narrow down the caller's need or problem through question-and-answers (the answers provided by pressing a button) with the end result simply some recorded information shared with the caller or a message saying that a response is being initiated automatically. Only in the case of the most persistent caller, who wades through all of these electronic options and bypasses them, is the option given to wait on the line for a service representative to answer the call.

Needless to say these automated systems are not highly popular with the public — though they are generally preferable to being kept silently on hold for long periods of time. In organizations where keeping callers happy and satisfied is more important, a second type of system is used to segregate calls into categories. The corporation issues a longer and more complicated set of phone listings that breaks down the various departments and services into separate phone numbers. The caller can then dial the department directly and have the phone answered by someone in that department. In some cases there is still a "general information" number for those who do not know exactly whom or what department they should be contacting. The person who answers these calls is a general switchboard operator who can redirect calls to other departments in the old style. However, because the other departments are listed and can be contacted separately, the volume of calls that need to go through the switchboard operator is generally reduced.

When companies use this system, with separate phone numbers for each department, it is often the department's administrative assistant who is the first one to answer the call. This is particularly likely when the department is small enough that only a handful of separate lines or extensions are needed to channel the calls to the various managers or others within the department. If the department is larger and answering calls is more or less a full-time assignment, there will be a departmental switchboard operator who is the first responder.

There are two additional evolutions in corporate phone systems worth mentioning here. The first is the advent of toll-free phone numbers. These are numbers by which a long distance call can be placed at the expense of the receiver of the call rather than the party who places it. Many firms offer toll-free numbers for customers wishing to place orders, service or help desk calls, and other purposes. Companies will have policies on how their staff is to handle these calls in order to keep costs under control. A lot depends on the nature of the arrangement the company has with its phone service provider. If these calls are billed by the minute like conventional long distance service, it becomes important to keep the calls as brief as possible without defeating the purpose of the service by antagonizing clients rather than providing them with an incentive for calling. However, it is becoming increasingly possible for companies to obtain very favorable rates for their toll-free service. In such cases the length of the phone call is less significant in terms of phone charges, but it still matters, because the time of the employees who answer these special phone lines can also be a significant cost factor. As labor costs start to outweigh the telephone charges, many large corporations are moving their service departments to foreign countries where workers are paid lower wages in comparison to North American rates and currencies. It might seem absurd for a U.S. or Canadian corporation to have toll free lines answered by employees working in a foreign country, but this is actually becoming an increasingly common reality in today's globalized world.

As you no doubt know from your own home telephone service, it is increasingly possible, both residentially and corporately, to obtain long distance rates that allow "unlimited" calling, either all the time, or during certain portions of the day. These plans make using long distance a more cost effective method of business communications than they once were.

A further evolution in this regard is the advent of voice-over-Internet protocol or VoIP phone service. As the name implies, this system routes calls from special phone sets into the company's computer system and from there through its Internet connection. The result is that long distance calling emulates email — unlimited use for a flat fee. This is a relatively new technology, but it is clearly the wave of the future for both residential and business use. It may well tip the scale away from email back toward the telephone as the primary means of business communications.

Having brought up the Internet, it is worth mentioning some other devices that allow office personnel to make use of the Internet and/or personal computers or computerized telecommunications equipment in order to send and receive both pictures and sound during live telecommunication conversations. Picture phones of various types have

been around for a while, and the technology changes so fast that any particular system will be obsolete almost as fast as one can publish information about it. Until recently the fact that both parties needed to have equipment capable of sending and receiving video as well as audio signals meant that picture phones were used more in business settings than by consumers. Their main business application was setting up "virtual conferences", where participants from remote locations could participate in a meeting both visually as well as audibly. As you may well be aware, the advent of cell phones that also transmit video has made this technology a reality for consumers also.

Another device now available to both consumers and businesses is the web cam. Web cams stream live video or video and audio. They are used by consumers for many purposes, but they can also be used by businesses for meetings, conferences, even for training purposes. One favorable point about web cams, or other devices that make use of the Internet is that the party who wishes to view and listen doesn't need any special equipment, other than a PC.

This text is designed for administrative assistants, not switchboard operators or call center specialists. It is therefore assumed that answering the telephone will be an important part of your job, but not close to being your entire job. That being the case, the telephone equipment you are apt to have on your desk will not be overly complex. It may typically give you the option of answering three or four different lines within the department and rerouting calls between them. Therefore, this is the scenario we will concentrate on in the rest of this section.

Business Telephone Features

At one time not so long ago it would have been a much bigger process of transition to learn the features of a typical business phone system after only having had experience with a residential phone. Most of the extra features of the business system might have been quite foreign to you at first. However, residential phone systems are now equipped with many of the features of business systems. Most householders are already familiar with such options as voice mail, answering more than one line, screening callers with caller ID, and cordless phone sets and/or speakerphones. However, it is still worth reviewing these basic features because there are additional considerations when using a business phone system.

Voice Mail

Voice mail is the electronic replacement for the telephone answering machine. When a person can't or doesn't wish to answer the phone, the voice mail answers automatically after a specified number of rings. The system broadcasts an outgoing message, and then offers the caller the opportunity to leave a recorded message. Unlike answering machines, voice mail is also activated when the person being called is presently on the line with another caller.

The obvious applications for voice mail are when a person is not at their desk, occupied with another call, or gone for the day, as well as to allow messages to be left after hours. However, many business people use voice mail for other purposes as well. One application is for screening calls. Many business phone systems display the number, and sometimes the name, of a caller while the phone is ringing. If the person does not wish to speak with the caller at this time (or at all) letting the voice mail system handle the call is one way of accomplishing this. Since the caller cannot know for sure whether the person being called is available to take the call or not, the caller doesn't generally feel rebuffed — unless this procedure is repeated several times and messages left on the system are not returned. However, letting voice mail handle a call in a system where caller ID is not available can be a risky venture. It could be your manager calling, or the president of the company, and the person might know that you are (or should be) at your desk. Most companies, or individual department managers, have policies with regard to screening calls and/or allowing voice mail to take calls that could be answered directly, and it is important for you to follow these procedures at all times.

There is another increasingly popular use of voice mail that affects administrative assistants in particular. It is often used to leave short business-related messages and reminders. Managers who work late often call their administrative assistant's line, despite knowing that the assistant is gone for the day, in order to record brief notes or reminders about various items that must be completed the next day. It is often much faster and simpler to do this than write a note and leave it on the assistant's desk. Also, it can be done after the manager has also gone home for the evening, or even while the manager is away on a business trip. Furthermore, it is not at all uncommon for administrative assistants and other office personnel to phone their own extension number when they are out of the office, and leave themselves a short reminder about something they may have forgotten to do or needs attending

to the following day. Once the assistant arrives at work, these messages can either be acted upon immediately, or transcribed into written notes and reminders for later on.

Call Forwarding

This is an example of a feature that people are less likely to set up on their residential phones, although it is available. Call forwarding allows your calls to be transferred automatically to another phone within the company if you do not wish to miss your calls while you are away from your desk. If you are expecting an important call and you want to answer it you can use this option. It is also frequently used by workers who receive a lot of important calls from other colleagues in the course of a day and want to be accessible rather than play "telephone tag" via the voice mail message system. As an administrative assistant you might find that your manager wants you to use call forwarding when you will be away from your desk for an extended period — or the manager may use the system to have calls forwarded to you in some situations.

Call Pick Up

This is a feature commonly used by administrative assistants who are responsible for answering other phones within the department, in addition to their own line or local extension. Call pick up can be programmed so that anyone within a designated group or department may answer a call for a colleague or manager who is not available at the time. Your manager and others in the department will have policies for when they want you to answer their phones and when they prefer to do so themselves.

Call Transfer

This feature allows you to answer a call and speak with the caller, then transfer the call to another extension within the company.

Conference Calls

The conference call feature allows more than two parties to be on the same line and participate in a call at the same time. This feature is used in order to invite colleagues at other telephone extensions within the system or at other phone numbers outside of the system, to join in a call. Conference calls can be used to handle problems, but they are also often used routinely for scheduled meetings when it is not practical for all participants to gather physically in the same room. Some conference calls are large and complex undertakings involving many different parties. Procedures for setting up these calls vary depending on the phone system in use and company policies, but they must be followed very precisely.

Speakerphones

Speakerphones allow for hands free use of a telephone. Most speakerphones are two-way — meaning that when the speakerphone function is activated the caller can hear you and you can hear the caller without actually lifting the telephone handset from the cradle. However, you will sometimes find one-way type speakerphones where you can hear, but the other party cannot hear you. These aren't true speakerphones in that they don't allow you to speak without lifting the handset. However, the speakers can be useful for hands free call screening or playing back voice mail messages.

Speakerphones are often used as an alternative to placing a conference call when two or more parties are able to gather together in the same room, but one or more participants cannot do so and must participate by phone. The speakerphone allows the absent participant to hear what is being discussed and join the discussion.

It is a courtesy to let callers know that they are on speakerphone and there is the possibility that someone else may overhear what is being said. At any time during a conversation it is

possible to pick up the handset, thereby deactivating the speaker, and turn the call into a private two-way conversation.

Redial and Ring Again

These two features are useful if you receive a busy signal when placing a call (which happens less and less frequently in this day of voice mail systems) or if you wish to place a second call to the same number you last dialed, whether or not that call was answered. Redial is simply a feature that saves time. When the redial button is pressed the phone calls the last number you dialed. Ring again is a more complicated feature. It is designed to be used when you receive a busy signal. When you activate the ring again feature, the phone system will monitor the line of the party you were trying to call. As soon as the line becomes free you will receive a special audio signal alerting you to this fact. When you pick up the handset, the phone system will dial the number for you. This saves the frustration of placing the same call over and over again only to discover that the line is still busy.

Speed Dial

Many people use this feature on their home phones as well as at work. It allows you to program numbers that you call frequently so that you can place calls to these numbers more rapidly, either by pushing a single button, or by entering a one- or two-digit number rather than a full phone number.

Supplementary Telephone-Based Systems

Today's business environment relies heavily on communications and the ability to contact or be contacted by anyone, anywhere, at any time. Some business people become so addicted to their communications equipment that they carry some sort of communicator with them wherever they go and keep it activated on a 24-7 basis. While often this serves a useful business purpose it can truly become an addiction, not to mention a source of stress for the businessperson and others. It is sometimes difficult to get people to turn off their cell phones or other devices in restaurants, movie theaters, or while onboard aircraft.

Rarely is an administrative assistant expected to be connected continuously inside and outside of the office. However, as a future administrative assistant you should know a little something about this supplementary equipment and how it is used.

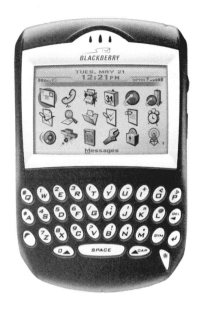

The main items in this category are cell phones, pagers, and personal computing devices such as The Blackberry. Most people are familiar with the basic functions and options for cell phones, and business cell phones are not fundamentally different from those available to consumers. However, business users tend to buy the most sophisticated cell phones available. Some of these have additional features besides the ability to place and receive phone calls. For example, they can be used for text messages, as walkie-talkies, and even for simple Internet connections. The walkie-talkie feature allows instant communications with one or more other phone users who are set up to be linked to the caller's walkie-talkie program. For example, if a manager and an administrative assistant both have cell phones with a walkie-talkie feature, it is possible for the manager to use the cell phone as an intercom to instantly contact and begin speaking with the assistant without the need to dial a phone number and wait for the call to be answered.

Pagers are used to send simple text messages. Their main role is not to complete a lengthy communication, but rather to contact a party and inform them that someone is trying to get in touch. The person with the pager will then generally phone the party who placed the page using either a cell phone or the conventional phone system. Pagers contain a small display screen that shows a phone number or a short text message. They can be clipped onto a belt and set to vibrate rather than ring, so that a message can be sent to someone who is in a location where telephone ringing would be frowned upon. However, their use is still prohibited in places where the radio signal they receive can cause interference with some local equipment or systems.

Email Systems

Email is a system for sending written messages from one computer to another by means of the Internet. Sometimes these messages are short and simple, but various types of documents, photographs, or other digital items can be attached to these messages, and in this way the email system can be used for transmitting significant amounts

of data. As a future administrative assistant you can expect that any employer where you may find yourself working will provide you with a computer that has Internet access. It is simply a must in today's business world.

There are various ways that the Internet connection to your office computer can be achieved. The connection may be through a line or cable, or it may be wireless. The specific connection method doesn't have a great effect on how to use the system. However, it can have an effect on the speed of transmission. This can be important when sending large quantities of data as email attachments. While some residential users still have the old-fashioned dial-up internet connections using low-speed phone lines, again in a modern office you can presume that you will have a high-speed connection.

For the average user email is conducted using the same office computer equipment that is used for preparing documents and other routine office tasks. Today, computers come with everything you will need to connect to the Internet and conduct email messaging. Thus, there are no new physical "gadgets" for you to learn about. Rather, you need to learn how to use the email software that is part of your computer's operating system.

Most business-based email is provided via an Internet Service Provider or through an internal network. Your computer must be specifically connected to this computer or network for you to access the email service. However, there is an alternative form of email of which you should be aware. This is known as web-based email. It is offered by companies such a Yahoo and Hotmail. Users of this system open accounts and register email user names with these

websites, usually free of charge. All email is managed through the provider's website. In other words, messages that you send and receive are stored on the provider's computer until you delete them. This is in contrast to the regular type of email, in which the Inbox and Sent Items folders that hold your old messages are stored on your own computer. Web-based email offers a few advantages. Until recently it was the only easy way that people could use their email service when they were away from their own computers. Because the web-based email is on the provider's computer, you can activate it from any computer with an Internet connection. You simply log on to the provider's website and enter a password, which allows you to access your account. However, in recent years it has become possible for users of other types of email services to also access the service from a computer other than their own. This is particularly easy to arrange at large companies that have their own networks. Nonetheless, there are still many email users who do not have this option. They need to be at the computer from which their email account was originally established in order to access the account.

A second advantage of web-based email is that, again because the messages are on someone else's s computer, you can often find an alternative way to access them if your own computer or local network goes down due to a maintenance failure, virus, machine damage, machine theft, or other problem. Web-based email is more limited than regular email with regard to the size of files you can transmit and the amount of storage space you are allowed to use for old messages. For this reason, it would be unusual for a business to use only web-based email. However, some of the clients or contacts with whom you will interact on the job may do so.

Whatever the means by which the system is connected and based, routine use of email is pretty much the same for all users. You need some type of software that allows your computer to function as an email sender and receiver. For most business users, their email software is part of their basic Windows operating system. For conventional email, the portion of the operating system called Outlook Express is often the email program. Web-based users must first connect to the website of the provider, often using Window's Internet Explorer. Once they have done that, they use the provider's software program. It may have a slightly different appearance, but it performs all the same basic functions as Outlook Express, so once you learn how to work in Outlook Express you can easily adapt to another format. Therefore, in this chapter we will profile Outlook Express as a typical example.

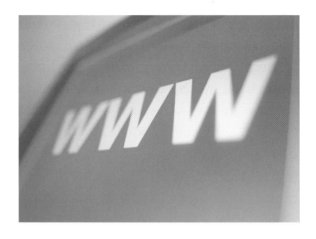

Without going into the details of what buttons to push and when, it is helpful to have an overall understanding of how a format like Outlook Express works. Many people will have had previous experience from home or school use, so we will keep our summary to just a brief refresher.

What you see when you first click on Outlook Express depends on how you have set up the program on your own computer. Many users go directly to their Inbox. This is a folder that holds all the messages the user has received since first using the program, minus any that were deliberately deleted. It is possible to accumulate literally thousands of email messages over time, unless you take periodic steps to delete some of them — which you should do from time to time. When you first go to the Inbox, you will see a list of messages. Each message shows the title that was given to the message by the sender, the sender's actual name or email name, and a symbol that indicates whether or not it contains attachments. Messages that you have not opened and read yet are bolded. When you click on the title of the message, the text of the message is displayed in a larger box below the list box. To open and read an email attachment you must separately click on the symbol for the attachment.

Other folders in Outlook Express (and other similar programs) include Sent Items, Deleted Items, Drafts and Outbox. As the name implies, the Sent Items folder stores all messages you have sent to other people until you choose to delete them. The Deleted Items file is really a second chance option in case you delete a message and then later decide that you still need it after all. The first time you delete a message it goes into the Deleted Items folder. However, if you then open the Deleted Items folder and delete a message a second time, it is truly deleted.

There are various reasons to delete messages once you are certain you no longer have any use for them. Although even a large number of email messages takes up relatively little space on a computer hard drive, cleaning up unwanted files of any kind provides storage space. More importantly, deleting old messages eliminates the risk that someone else will find and open them at a later date. This applies both to personal messages and business-related messages of a sensitive nature. The final reason for deleting old emails is that it makes it easier to find those you do need to keep. Searching for an old message among hundreds or thousands of emails can be a tedious task, although there are ways to speed up the search.

The Outbox is a special folder about which you should know a little something. In most cases there will be nothing in your Outbox. When you send a message it enters the Outbox very briefly, usually for just a few seconds or less, while it is in the process of being transmitted. However, occasionally a message that you try to send cannot go out over the network for one reason or another. The internal network or external email service provider may be experiencing technical difficulties. There may also be a temporary problem with your own computer, or it may be in the process of performing a task that is taking most of its computing power. Any time you

message back or prevent the recipient from opening it. Using the Draft folder allows you to double-check messages before sending them, or work on longer or more complicated messages in more than one sitting.

notice that a message is still in your Outbox, you know it has not yet been sent. Most computers are set up so that they will keep trying to send messages in the Outbox automatically, without any specific action on your part. As soon as the computer is successful in completing the transmission, the message will disappear from your Outbox and be relocated to Sent Items.

The Draft folder allows you to work on messages and save them without yet sending them. Sometimes it is important to put careful thought into the content or wording of an important message. One danger with email is that it prompts some people to be a bit hasty. The moment you click the Send button there is no way to get the

Chapter 2

MANAGING INCOMING AND OUTGOING
Communications

Telephone Procedures and Techniques

In the previous section we detailed the common features of modern office telephone systems. In this part of the text we will go into greater detail on how to use these features, both from a technical perspective, and in terms of achieving effective communications that conform with necessary standards of etiquette, security, and efficiency.

Because actual telephone equipment varies by type of system, make, and

model, we cannot specify the exact sequence of buttons to push. You will have to learn those finer details during your orientation to the specific administrative assistant position for which you are eventually hired. However, apart from the specifications of what the controls look like, there is some general standardization with regard to the sequence of procedures and accepted practices. Even here you will naturally have to defer to the specific policies and preferences of your employer. However, by becoming familiar with the overall sequence of a typical operation, you will achieve a significant head start that should greatly accelerate your learning curve on the job and make you more useful to your employer sooner than someone without this background.

Before we start reviewing typical procedural sequences, it is worth taking a second to clarify what the general objectives are in the management of telephone communications in the office setting. You will better appreciate the significance of procedural do's and don'ts if you realize that they are designed to facilitate meeting the following goals:

- achieving communications that are as efficient as possible in terms of cost and staff time

- giving employees in general, and managers in particular, a suitable degree of control over how they handle ongoing communications so that company objectives are furthered and not hindered by these communications

- preserving confidentiality and decorum through the professional routing and control of calls

- providing a satisfactory communications experience for the outside caller in a way that solidifies and maximizes the caller's positive experience of communicating with the company, and therefore the caller's inclination to continue a positive relationship with the company

Every phone call that comes into a company from someone on the outside of the organization presents both an opportunity and a risk. The opportunity obviously varies depending on the nature of the call and the caller. In some cases there is the opportunity to make a sale. However, even when that is not the case, there is always the opportunity to leave the caller with a positive image of the company that will influence the caller's future behavior toward the company in tangible and intangible ways. The risks are, first, that this will fail to happen, and worse, that the communication will result in the caller being placed in a position and/or given the inclination to harm the company in some way. This can occur through the leaking of confidential information, or through a rude or unprofessional experience that causes hostility. This can result in anything from taking the company to court, at one extreme, to simply grumbling to peers about the bad experience.

Negative occurrences during telephone communications are a bit like traffic accidents. 99% of the time things progress normally, then suddenly out of nowhere a mistake is made and harm occurs, often before the parties are aware of what is happening and the likely repercussions. Because no one can be fully attentive and anticipatory 100% of the time, good phone habits, like good driving habits, need to become engrained in staff members in order to give them the best possible chance of avoiding as many mistakes as possible, and catching and correcting those that do occur.

Answering Calls

From a technical standpoint, answering a telephone call is probably the simplest of all telephone procedures. In most

cases all you need to do is pick up the handset and speak. However, if there is more than one line that passes through your phone, you may first need to push the button that answers the specific line. This is usually indicated by a flashing light.

Calls should generally be answered after the second or third ring. Answering after the first ring may catch the caller off guard. However, many voice mail systems are set to take the call after the fourth or fifth ring, so you should answer the call before that happens. Even if there is no voice mail system callers tend to get frustrated and give up after too many rings.

While the procedure is simple, the task itself can be deceptively complex from a different point of view. The first words you say when answering a call coming through on a company line are critically important to establishing a professional image and tone, as well as to route the call toward efficient communication and resolution. The specific first words you use will often be dictated by company policy, and they will depend on the nature of the business line you are answering, as well as the identity of the caller.

In some cases where administrative assistants may answer more than one line, they are expected to extend a different greeting depending on which line is answered. Coordinating these greetings can be challenging, especially when the phone rings often or interrupts you in the midst of something else. One thing you must avoid is the "stammering greeting". Examples, "Good morn — I mean, good afternoon"... "Hello- I mean, Service Department — how can I help you?" When you prepare to answer a phone call, take a breath, and use the pause to collect your thoughts and turn your attention to the call itself. A delay of a second or two before speaking is much better than a hurried greeting. Sometimes a caller can detect hurriedness or frustration in the voice of a person answering a call, and it can put the caller on the defensive, or create hesitancy or confusion.

Here are some other important general guidelines for answering phones and greeting callers.

• Speak slowly and clearly. Your voice must convey warmth and welcome, as well as a sense of calm and control. Admittedly sometimes this will require a bit of acting when a call comes in at an inopportune moment. Always remember, that is never the caller's fault. Never misdirect frustration from some other cause toward a caller. Also, even if things are hectic at the moment, try not to make it sound that way. Remember that you are a representative of your company, and you are putting forward a corporate image to the caller. People are reluctant to deal with organizations or departments that appear to be poorly organized, or swamped with other responsibilities. That may be the situation at this particular moment, but the caller may not understand that this is not the way things usually are, and may jump to conclusions about the firm's organization, friendliness, or competency.

• Never assume that you know who is calling or what the caller wants. Give the proper greeting in all cases. Many people get caught expecting an imminent phone call from one party, but before that party manages to complete the call, a different call slips in from another caller. If you pick up the phone and start talking to the person you think is calling, there will be confusion and embarrassment when the person who is actually on the phone has to interrupt you and point out your mistaken assumption. Phones that have caller ID reduce this risk in some cases, but even then it is wise not to make assumptions. Someone could be calling you from someone else's line or extension. You may find it monotonous at times, but extend the proper greeting all the time, in keeping with company and departmental policies.

• At times it may be necessary to place a caller on hold. No caller enjoys this experience, but some reasons for being placed on hold are more acceptable than others. For example, callers don't necessarily mind being put on hold for a reasonably brief interval while you search for information for them, or activate the process of transferring their call to another department. What callers DON'T like is being placed on hold so you can answer another call or conclude some conversation with someone else, especially if it happens more than once during the conversation, or if they are placed on hold immediately after their call is answered before they have had a chance to speak. If a caller is placed on hold for more than a few seconds they are unable either to achieve the objective of the call or to conclude it. In this era of voice mail it is not a good idea to answer a call if all you can do is immediately place the caller on indefinite hold. At least if they get the voice mail they will quickly be able to leave a message if they wish and terminate the call. People resign themselves to long waits whenever they have to phone the tax department to request a form, or a public utility to inquire about a service interruption. However, in the case of a competitive business engaged in general commerce, the tolerance/resignation level may be rather low — particularly if they are accustomed to receiving more prompt and courteous service from the company's competitors.

On occasion you will have no choice but to place a caller on hold. While you need to learn and respect your employer's and your manager's policies and preferences for such situations, here are some general guidelines for how to minimize the risk of irritating the caller or losing the call:

• Whenever possible ask the caller's permission to place the caller on hold, and stay on the line long enough to receive an answer.

• Avoid placing callers on hold for extended periods of time. What constitutes an "extended period of time" depends on the situation. However, unless you are manning a phone line where callers would expect a heavy volume of calls, anything much over 15 seconds is a long wait, especially if the caller has not had a chance to state the purpose of the call. Even after you have begun to assist the caller a wait of longer than one minute while you accomplish something on behalf of the caller can grow irritating.

• If you know that you are going to have to leave the caller on hold longer than this, you have a couple of options. The first, of course, is not to answer the call at all and let it be handled by voice mail. The second is to give the caller an idea of how long a delay to expect, the reason for the delay, and ask if the caller is willing to wait or would prefer to call back or be called back.

• When a wait is longer than you expected or intended, you should get back on the line after the time stated in the guideline and once again offer the caller the option of continuing to wait or postponing the call to another time. This rule also applies when you are waiting to transfer a caller to another line that is currently busy. Too many people in this situation make the mistake of placing the caller on hold and then forgetting about them, failing to notice after a minute or two, or longer, that the line is still busy and that the caller is still on hold. Particularly when a person is calling long distance they may be willing to endure a short wait, but not an extended one. If you place a caller on hold too

swiftly, and then fail to return to check on the caller after some time has passed, you may not give the caller the chance to explain that the call is long distance and/or urgent in nature — facts that will further increase the caller's sense of frustration with remaining on hold.

• In addition to returning to check on the caller, always apologize for the wait. The wait may not be your fault, but the apology is a courtesy. It shows that you sympathize with the caller's frustration at being placed on hold.

• Whenever you have kept a caller waiting for you, when you do take or resume the call, go out of your way to make sure that you give the caller your undivided time and attention, and do your best to resolve the caller's need or issue.

• Unless it is absolutely unavoidable, never ask the caller to endure two extended waits in the course of a single phone call. There is nothing more frustrating to a caller than having endured a wait, only to be interrupted and put on hold a second time.

• This is a tough one, but no matter the situation, avoid sounding rushed or panicked. Some employees in this situation seem to think that if they blurt out their requests or statements about the need to place the caller on hold in a frantic tone, the caller will better appreciate how truly busy they are. This is the wrong approach. It might take you four or five seconds to ask the caller to hold in a rushed tone of voice, and seven or eight seconds to make the same request more calmly and cordially. In most cases it is well worth adding the extra two or three seconds than to treat the caller with discourtesy.

Placing Calls

Placing phone calls is also a simple procedure technically. If more than one line is handled through your phone set, you may have to select a line button, then proceed with the call, or simply dial 9 to get an outside line.

In many organizations the procedure for placing a call varies slightly depending on whether it is an inside or outside call. If you are calling someone else within the organization, sometimes all you need to do is dial a four-digit number for the other internal party. If the company has a more complicated system and not all internal extensions have the same prefix, sometimes you may need to dial a full seven-digit code. In most cases when you wish to dial a local or long distance number outside of the company's internal phone system you must begin your call by dialing 9. In some cases after doing so you must wait a moment to hear a second, different type of dial tone before dialing the outside number. You would then dial the outside number in the same way you would dial from your home phone. If it is a long distance call within North America you must dial 1, then the area code, then the number. If it is an overseas call you must dial the proper international prefix.

When placing long distance calls to other parts of the country or internationally, it is very important to keep track of time zones. There are four time zones within the United States, and six within Canada. Remember that places east of you are ahead of you in time whereas places to the west of you are behind. Most parts of Western Europe are five or six hours ahead of Eastern Standard Time (i.e. New York). For other destinations you should consult a standard time zone chart. You will find one in the front of most telephone directories and on the internet. When a company does a lot of business with an office in another part of the world, sometimes separate clocks will be installed that show the current time in these other places to reduce the amount of mental calculations staff members need to make.

Transferring Calls

In the previous paragraphs we mentioned that the need to transfer a call is one situation in which you might briefly need to place a caller on hold. While the details of the procedure for transferring calls vary depending on the type of system and equipment in use, there are several important general guidelines for the normal sequence of events, as well as guidelines for helping to ensure that the process goes smoothly.

The first step is to familiarize yourself thoroughly with the company's phone system and procedures. This knowledge should be layered over your core knowledge of the company itself, its organizational structure, and the functions of key departments and staff members to whom it is most probable

that you will need to redirect calls. You will annoy callers if you botch the technical aspects of transferring the call, but they won't be any happier if you smoothly transfer them to the wrong department or extension.

The transfer procedure itself may vary depending on the destination of the call and how that destination line or extension is related to your line within the telephone system. There are two main possibilities:

1) You need to transfer the call to a different line within your own department, a line that is available at your phone and that you have direct access to answering. This isn't a true transfer, because in many cases the caller can stay on the same line on which the call originated. You simply need to place the caller on hold, contact a third party who also has access to that line, and have the third party pick up the call. The way you will contact the third party varies depending on the equipment and policies in use. In some cases after putting the incoming caller on hold, you will call the office colleague from your line and inform the colleague that there is a call, and what line it is on. If the colleague agrees to take the call, you hang up. The colleague pushes the phone button that allows access to the line on which the caller is waiting, and can then speak directly to the caller.

2) You need to transfer the call to a different extension or line within the company, one that does not go through your phone. This is a true transfer because the call is being rerouted to a different line. The general procedure for doing this is as follows:

• Let the caller know that you are going to transfer the call.

• Press whatever control button on your phone is used to initiate the transfer. In many cases this is called the Transfer button or the Forward button. Pressing this button places the caller on hold, and you hear a dial tone in your handset.

• Dial the number or extension code of the third party to whom you wish to redirect the call. Depending upon the size of the organization and how the phone lines are set up, this may be a two-digit extension number or a four-digit extension number. Sometimes in systems that assign separate 7-digit phone numbers to all departments and most staff members, the last four digits can be used for placing calls within the company's local network or for transferring calls.

• What you do next depends on what happens when the system contacts the phone of the party to whom you wish to transfer the call. If the line is free and that person answers the phone, speak with the third party and announce your intention to transfer the call. If the person agrees to receive the call, press the Transfer button a second time.

• Usually there is a final step to complete the transfer and free your own phone line from the process. There may be a Release button, or a similar button that you need to press before replacing your own handset in the cradle. The purpose of the Release button is to achieve a prompt disconnect of your line from the trunk.

- If you receive a busy signal, you need to return to the caller with the information that you are unable to complete the transfer at this time. There will be a button on your phone to achieve this purpose. On some systems this is the main button that taps you into your own personal line or extension.

Note: In an office that is set up for voice mail, whenever a line is occupied, any new call will usually go automatically to the voice mail system. In many systems, however, the voice mail does not kick in during an internal transfer procedure. You receive a busy signal instead. If the line is busy, return to the caller and then, depending on company policy, ask the caller if they would like to hold, or explain how to call the third party's line directly, in which case the caller will be able to try later, and will have the option of leaving a voice mail message.

What should generally be avoided, if possible, is any situation that will require the caller to remain on hold indefinitely, or that will obligate you to make repeated attempts to transfer the call. You have no way of knowing how long a colleague's phone line will be occupied. Remember that callers on hold are helpless — their only option is to hang up. If they have not yet been given information about how to contact the party that can help them directly, they will then have to call you again, and start the process all over again. They may not do this, either out of frustration, or perhaps embarrassment at having lost patience and hung up the previous time. In either case the company could end up losing an important call. Remember: the caller is your responsibility until such time as you successfully complete the transfer or return to the line and reach some agreement with the caller to end the call. It is easy to lose track of callers on hold, particularly if you have to answer one or more other calls in the meantime, or are interrupted by some other duty.

Occasionally callers waiting on hold get "cut off". This can happen if you accidentally press a wrong button (or if someone else with access to the line does). It can also happen due to a technical glitch or a momentary overload in the system. This is an embarrassing and awkward eventuality, all the more so because the caller can never be sure whether it was accidental or deliberate.

A useful extra step when taking and transferring calls in systems that have caller I.D. is to make a note of the caller's phone number before initiating the transfer. In that case if a call should become lost in the system or accidentally disconnected, either you or the person to whom the call was destined may be able to phone the caller back, apologize for the mix up, and get the call back on track. Company policies vary on whether or not you should ask who is calling before initiating a transfer.

Most companies will establish protocol and etiquette regarding announcing a call transfer to a third party. In some companies you may be expected to identify yourself to your colleague and then inform the colleague that you are transferring a call (if you are expected to attempt to get the name of the caller, you would also pass along this information). Other companies find that this simply prolongs the transfer

process at the caller's expense, and prefer a more succinct transfer announcement. Furthermore, in some systems you do not actually speak to the person to whom you are transferring the call. In such a case there may be little point in collecting information about the caller, since you have no way to pass it along to your colleague.

Although almost all corporate phone systems are set up for transferring calls, some managers gently discourage use of the procedure. It is sometimes preferable to tell the caller the name of the department and/or specific staff member to whom they should be speaking, and then give the caller that phone number, asking the caller to please hang up and call back directly. Besides saving you a little bit of time, an advantage of this approach is that you are sure that callers know with whom they should be speaking and how to get in touch with them in the future. If you transfer the call for the caller, they may fail to take note of this information. If the caller accidentally becomes disconnected, or needs to place a second call to the same party, the caller may become dependent on you to transfer the call. The other advantage is that in many cases this will be the only way that the caller can access the third party's voice mail system, since transfers that do not go through sometimes do not provide access to voice mail. Nonetheless, sometimes a caller will ask you to transfer the call. For example, a caller dialing from a pay phone or long distance may understandably not wish to start over again and place a second phone call. For this reason, the transfer option should be made available.

In some large organizations not all calls can be transferred. There may be a department that is on a completely separate phone system, perhaps because they are located in a different facility. In such cases you will have no choice but to explain to the caller that you are unable to transfer the call, and instruct the caller on how to place the call directly.

Setting Up a Conference Call

On many office phone systems the procedure for setting up a conference call is very similar to that of transferring a call. However, instead of using the Transfer or Forward button, there is often a separate button called Conference (or a similar name). The difference between the effects of a Conference and a Transfer button is that the Conference button keeps you on the line, whereas a Transfer button is designed to sever your connection once the third party has come onto the line. Otherwise, the basic procedure is usually similar to what we already covered for call transferring. Pressing

the Conference button will put the original caller on hold and give you a dial tone so you can dial the extension of a third party. Once you receive an answer, pressing the Conference button again results in all three parties being connected. This procedure can then be repeated to add one or more additional parties to the call, although there is often a maximum number that can be included. Note: most major employers these days have conference call capability built into their telephone system. However, for those who don't, long distance conference calls can sometimes be set up by a conference call operator at your company's long distance provider.

Conference calls are usually initiated with advance notice. In most cases you don't want to be explaining the purpose of the call and getting a colleague's agreement to participate once other callers are already on the line and waiting. These calls tend to be scheduled ahead of time so that all parties are prepared and the lines can be kept free.

When scheduled conference calls involve managers or executives, sometimes administrative assistants are expected to set up the calls, then let the executives know when they may pick up the line and participate. In some cases a group of administrative assistants activate the call and come on the line together, then turn the call over to their respective managers. Depending on the telephone and communications system in place, once the administrative assistant has everything in order for the call, the assistant informs the manager either by placing the conference call on hold and dialing the manager's extension, by informing the manager via an intercom system, or sometimes simply by walking into the manager's office to say the call is ready. Transferring a conference call to another line can be tricky, so it is generally best to start the call from the line the manager will be using to participate. In an office where the manager's extension and the administrative assistant's extension can both be accessed from either person's desk, it is much simpler for the assistant to place the call from his or her own desk, and then have the manager come on simply by picking up his or her handset and pushing the line button for the extension on which the call has been placed.

We will take a moment here to talk in general about the administrative assistant placing calls on behalf of the manager. At one time it was fairly common in the business world for business executives and managers to have their "secretaries" routinely place outgoing calls for them, get the desired party on the line, and then inform the manager to pick up the call. The situation would begin with the manager contacting the secretary by phone or intercom with a request such as "Please get Peter Miller on the line for me." The secretary would then phone Mr. Miller's office. The secretary there would answer and be told something like, "Mr. Rodgers is calling for Mr. Miller." Mr. Miller's secretary would then determine whether or not Mr. Miller was willing and able to take the call. What happened next would sometimes depend on the rank or status of the two parties. If Mr. Rodger was Mr. Miller's superior, Mr. Miller would be expected to come on the line first, and then wait while Mr. Rodgers' secretary got him to pick up the line. If the reverse was true, or Mr. Miller was a client of Mr. Rodgers' firm, then once Mr. Miller agreed to take the call, Mr. Rodgers' secretary would ask Mr. Rodgers to come on the line first, and he would wait for Mr. Miller to pick up. The assumption seemed to be that the "more important" party would not be asked to wait on the line for the other (and that the time of both parties was more important than that of their secretaries, who would have to stop what they were doing in order to get these two men connected). All of this served little purpose other than "status boosting", and the practice has largely been discontinued. Occasionally you will find a senior executive who asks an executive secretary to set up some phone calls in this way, but it is becoming rare.

One exception is that sometimes a manager will ask an administrative assistant to place an overseas call. Getting connected to an overseas line can be a longer and more tedious task, especially to some destinations, and a more significant and useful amount of the manager's time can be saved by having the assistant help in this regard. In most parts of the world long distance calls can be dialed directly without operator assistance, provided you know the complete phone number. Calls within North America and to many parts of the Caribbean can be dialed in the same way as any other long distance call within your own country. You must know the area code for that region, or you can look up the

area code in the front section of your phone book. Long distance calls to other countries overseas generally start with the international access code 011, followed by a country code, then a city or area code and the local number. You should be aware that it can take several extra seconds to be connected to an overseas call, although as technology continues to improve, waiting time is rapidly decreasing.

Not only has the practice of placing calls on behalf of someone else faded, but increasingly the practice of having incoming calls answered by someone else is also gradually disappearing. You will find more and more managers and executives these days who answer their own phones, and only ask administrative assistants to do so when they are busy or out of the office. The prestige thing is no longer as trendy, and with the advent of caller ID a manager doesn't need an assistant to screen incoming calls. He or she can usually see who is calling and elect to answer the call or let it go to voice mail.

Managing Voice Mail

Most offices today utilize a voice mail system and there are some routine tasks that must be performed to initiate and maintain the system. One responsibility is to record one or more greetings that will be heard by any caller who is routed to voice mail. You must follow company policy and your manager's wishes when scripting these greetings. If the line for which you are recording the message is assigned to you personally and listed in your name within the company, you may be expected to begin by greeting the caller then giving your own name and/or your title and/or the name of the department. To some extent the wording of your greeting will depend on whether or not the voice mail system itself greets the caller. For example, in some systems the computerized system informs callers that their call is being transferred to the voice mail system, then tells the caller they have reached the voice mail box of _____. You would record your name and/or title, and this is announced after the system message. However, if the system does not offer a standard greeting and explanation, then your message must greet the caller and state that the call has been transferred to voice mail. Be careful in such a case that your first words are not identical to what you would say if you answered the call. If the first word you say is "Hello" the caller may say hello back before realizing that you are not actually on the line.

When people record voice mail or answering machine messages personally at home, they are usually reluctant to state that they are not home, for fear that an unscrupulous caller might take this as an inducement to break into the home. People tend to leave vague messages to the effect that "they are unable to take the call at this moment." However, in an office setting one doesn't usually have this worry, so it is often helpful to record a more specific message. For example, many administrative assistants record a special voice mail message that is activated at the end of the work day, informing callers that the office is closed, letting them know what normal office hours are, and inviting callers to leave a message if they wish. If there is an emergency after-hours number, that number may also be given out in the message. Likewise, if a person will be away on holiday or business trip, often a special voice mail message will be recorded letting callers know how long you will be gone, and perhaps leaving the phone number or extension of someone else in the department who can assist the caller until you return.

During the day, the outgoing message may be the more general "away from my desk" or "unable to take your call at this time".

Passwords are needed in order to use any voice mail feature. This prevents other persons inside or outside of the company from gaining unauthorized access to your messages, or changing your outgoing message. You must enter your password before changing your greeting, and before retrieving any messages in your voice mail box.

Some companies ask administrative assistants to log all incoming calls, whether answered by a person or routed to the voice mail system. Others require only certain calls of a specific nature be logged. The log entry might typically include the name and number of the caller, and the time and nature of the call or message. The log can be kept via computer, using a paper logbook, or a message pad. It is also possible to save voice mail messages in the system after you have listened to them. In the case of a detailed message, this gives you the option of listening to a message a second time, either right away or later. You may wish to make notes regarding a detailed message, and it may be necessary to hear it more than once in order to accomplish this effectively.

Telephone Etiquette

Up to now we have described basic telephone procedures, while noting that exact procedural details vary somewhat depending on the system in use and the employer's policies. However, there is another aspect to effective telephone communications besides the technical one. It is very important for administrative assistants to develop an efficient, personable, and professional style of speaking with callers and helping them to fulfill the purpose of their calls. We cannot provide scripts for exactly what to say in every situation, but we can give you some important general guidelines that will have a broad range of applicability.

• To begin with, get to know your telephone equipment and system thoroughly. Practice with it, and pay attention to the fine details. For example, take note of the effects of changing the volume settings, and the degree to which background noises are picked up by the system. Take note of timing factors as well. Too many people manning office phones routinely chop the first or last syllables they say to callers by beginning to speak too quickly after picking up the handset, or pushing a button too quickly after completing a concluding statement. Take note of how close the transmitter microphone needs to be to your mouth — generally between one-half and one inch is best depending on the equipment.

• Always speak calmly and clearly. There is a special talent involved in appearing calm, cool, and collected when you are really not, but it is a talent you need to acquire. You should use a consistent tone and approach when answering phone calls, not one that varies depending on the mood of the day or the current situation surrounding you in the office at that moment.

• When appropriate, ask for and take note of important information identifying the caller. In many cases this includes the name of the caller, the company they are calling from, if any, and the caller's phone number. Listen carefully if the caller offers this information, and write it down. If you do not hear clearly ask the caller to repeat — but you shouldn't have to ask the caller to repeat the information simply because you weren't paying full attention at the start of the call. In most cases you should not ask the caller for spellings of names if you are merely transferring the call, but it is critically important to do so if you are taking a message. Whenever you must take a written message, confirm all spellings and numbers with the caller. Never guess. Even a common name can often have two or more possible spellings.

• In this era of voice mail, taking written phone messages on behalf of someone else is less common, but there will be situations in which you will be expected to do so, and many offices have printed message pads for this purpose. Be sure to request the information needed to complete all items on the message pad, unless the caller is already familiar to you and to the party he or she is trying to contact, or does not wish to provide certain information. Repeat key information to the caller, such as the caller's phone number or numbers. Depending on company policy and the nature of the call you may be expected to inquire as to the general nature or purpose of the call. However, unless the matter is something you are expected to handle yourself, avoid taking long and complicated written messages whenever possible unless the caller is insistent. If you do not completely understand the caller's issues, there is a risk you will misinterpret or misrecord some of the details. Also, it is pointless to let the caller give you details that you cannot or will not pass along to the third party, and callers dislike giving a full explanation to one person only to discover that they have to start all over again giving the same explanation to someone else. It is sometimes a good idea to ask the caller when would be a convenient time for the manager to return the call, but never commit your manager to returning the call at some specific time unless you are certain that the manager will be willing and able to do so. Always deliver a message promptly, and if a person is not in the office ensure that you place the message where it will be seen immediately upon the person's return. Some managers may instruct you to take written messages when the manager is in a meeting. You need to be clear on the manager's policy for delivering these messages. In some cases the manager may want you to enter the room quietly and give the manager the written message while the meeting is in progress. In other cases the manager will prefer that written messages be saved until the meeting has concluded.

• When taking a call for someone else, avoid divulging information about the manager or other third party on whose behalf you are speaking. You often don't know what the relationship is between the caller and the other party, and you should not make assumptions. You can promise to deliver a message, but you cannot promise that the other party will return the call. You should never disclose what the other party is presently doing, or what the other party's schedule is for the day — unless that party has given you permission to divulge such information.

• An incoming call is either your responsibility to handle or it isn't, and you either know the correct response to the caller's inquiry or you don't. Guesses, hunches, or theories on your part should never enter into the equation. Any statement on your part that includes the word "probably" is probably on thin ice from the start. If you are not certain about a piece of information — or that you ought to be sharing it with the caller — don't. Simply inform the caller that you do not have that information, but that you will give the message to the appropriate party. Whenever in doubt, particularly with a caller whom you do not know, be polite but take a cautious and conservative approach.

Handling Problem Calls

Apart from the technical side of the phone, and the aspect of etiquette, it is obviously also extremely important that administrative assistants be well trained in what to say on the phone, to ensure positive outcomes from interactions. All companies have policies about how inquiries should be handled or redirected. When you get a phone call from someone who doesn't appear to know to whom they should be speaking, the first step is to explore the fundamental nature or purpose of the inquiry. Is it a general request for information about products and services? Is it an inquiry from a customer about a transaction or account? Is it a complaint about some product, service, or interaction with the company? Or, perhaps the caller is a businessperson hoping to obtain information, or sell a product or service. If you aren't a perceptive listener who asks the appropriate questions, you may fail to grasp the basic nature of the

call, and that makes it almost impossible for you to respond to it appropriately. There are really only two basic rules of thumb when it comes to probing the nature of a call:

1) listen to the caller, without interrupting, and without trying to rush the interaction toward some premature conclusion; and

2) ask simple, direct, polite questions as to how you can be of assistance to the caller, or what the caller needs from you at this time.

Once you have ascertained the purpose of the call, follow company and departmental policy with regard to directing the call to the appropriate party. Handle those calls you are expected to handle, and refer those calls you are expected to refer.

Let us now turn our attention to calls whose nature appears to fall within your personal jurisdiction and expertise. Routine requests and interactions will be relatively easy to handle once you are up to speed on the nature of the work that is done in your department. However, your real test will come when something has gone wrong, and you must take a phone call that involves a problem, a complaint, or worse, an irate or abusive caller.

The first thing you need to understand and appreciate is that if the caller has a problem, you have a problem. You may not be the cause of the problem, and on occasion it may even seem unfair that it has been "dumped on your lap", but nonetheless here it is, and it is your responsibility to deal with it, or at least make a first attempt to do so. Even if the problem is based on a misunderstanding, and the true situation is not at all as the caller appears to perceive it, that misunderstanding itself is a problem. People are rarely totally irrational and unreasonable. If they have taken an adversarial stance it is because from their point of view, limited though that may sometimes be — they are suffering from some sort of wrong or harm that needs to be set right.

Experts in salesmanship often teach sales recruits that complaints are actually golden opportunities for any business. At first glance, this statement may leave you scratching your head. You have an angry or upset customer or inquirer on the line — how can this possibly be a good thing? Well, it isn't, not at the moment. However, good can come out of it if you handle the situation properly. When someone takes a caller's concern seriously and acts vigorously to resolve it and make things right, the caller comes away feeling relief, gratitude (and occasionally a bit of embarrassment or regret at having allowed oneself to get so upset in the first place). This combination of emotional reactions can actually build future loyalty toward the organization in general, and toward the staff member in particular who has been so effective in rallying to their cause.

Occasionally, however, you will be confronted with a truly unreasonable caller who will create a disagreeable situation from which no good can presently come. There is a considerable difference between a complaint, even an angry one, and a call that involves harassment, threats, or offensive language. Hopefully you will not often find yourself in such a situation, but if you ever do, follow these very important guidelines.

• In the case of a "crank call" where the caller is clearly looking for attention, will not divulge their identity, and does not appear to have any legitimate business, hang up. Don't give this ill-adjusted person any attention.

• If the caller makes a threat, or utters an obscene or abusive remark, understand that you are dealing with a criminal offense in progress, and respond accordingly. Remain calm, but do the following.

• Obtain as much information about the caller as you can. Naturally if your phone system has caller ID take written note of any information that is displayed.

• Make written notes of any other information that might help police identify the caller, such as speech patterns, background noise etc.

• Do not divulge any information to the caller that the caller does not already possess.

• Do not argue, or even try to reason with the caller — an abusive caller is not in a reasonable state of mind.

• Do not issue any threat or counter-threat against the caller.

• Unless you feel you have a chance of obtaining additional useful information, do not participate in or prolong the conversation: hang up.

• Immediately report the call to your supervisor, or to the corporate security office, or call the police — never presume that a threat of any kind is not a serious matter.

• If you have any reason to believe that the caller is angry with you personally, or has personal information about you, speak with the police about your own personal safety until such time as the criminal is apprehended.

Let's hope that you will never have to take these steps in the course of your working career. However, like preparation for any other type of emergency situation, it's a good idea to keep this information in the back of your mind so you will respond appropriately with the right instincts should such a situation ever arise.

Email Messages and Processes

Email is becoming *the* system today, not only for office communications, but also for delivery or dispersal of various documents. The procedural details on how to perform specific email tasks vary depending on the software in use at any particular employer, as well as that employer's policies and preferences. However, just as we did with telephone communications, without getting down to what buttons to push we can give you a good grounding in what is involved in these procedures. This information will make it easier for you when you move on to the computer training phase, as well as when you are learning employer-specific details once you are hired. In the following paragraphs we will first discuss handling incoming email messages. Then we will discuss how to generate them to send to others.

The first thing you need to understand about the text-creation part of email software is that it is similar to but separate from the word processing software you will use to prepare and save letters, reports and other forms of text. The differences affect the options you have while creating messages. Also, email messages you have already sent or received continue to be saved by your email software until such time as you act to delete them, but again, the types of files that contain these messages and your options for what you can do with them, are different from "regular" word-processed files. In general, your options are more limited when producing and storing email messages. The software is intended to give you capabilities you need for the specific purpose of sending and receiving text messages that will have a limited shelf life. Nonetheless, there is a compatibility between your email software and your word processing software. Documents produced using word processing software can be sent as email attachments, and as such they retain the full features and capabilities of the software that produced them. Also, text that is in the body of an email message, rather than sent as an attachment, can be copied and "pasted" into a word processing document.

The point we want to make is that unless you do something specific to save or copy material that you receive by email, it ends up in a system that is not really designed for safe and permanent storage. Thus, decisions need to be made about incoming email. In essence, each message needs to be assessed to one of three categories:

1) messages that are of no conceivable use to you after you have read them

2) messages that you would like to save for a short time, perhaps until you have had a chance to reply or until the matter is resolved, but that have no long-term use or significance

3) messages of which either the body of the message, or one or more attachments, or both, constitute important material that you want to save and use indefinitely or permanently.

The first type of message mentioned above can be deleted as soon as it is read, or as soon as it is replied to, if a reply is warranted. Whatever email software system you will be using, the messages will be displayed within an on-screen template with various clickable options, among them a delete button. Hitting the delete button sends the message to a Deleted Items folder. From there, repeating the procedure will delete the message permanently. Most other types of files that you may choose to delete go into a special area called the "Recycle Bin". If you change your mind later on you can go back into the Recycle Bin and retrieve them (until such time as you empty your bin). Items that you clear out of your Deleted Items email folder do not go to your Recycle Bin — they are simply erased. In a sense the "Deleted Items" folder IS the Recycle Bin for email messages.

Messages that you wish to keep for a short period of time (hours, days, or in some cases weeks) don't require any specific action on your part. Messages are stored in your Inbox until you take action to move them to another folder or delete them. Your Inbox is capable of holding hundreds or even thousands of messages, but it is unwise to let them accumulate to that degree. Once you are sure you have no further use for the message, you should delete it (which means that it disappears from your Inbox and simultaneously appears in your Deleted Items folder.) Then periodically you should clean out the Deleted Items folder as well. You can clean out your Deleted Items folder by deleting messages you select individually, or by using a "Delete All" option that deletes them all at once.

Messages that fit in the third category we have identified, items of ongoing or permanent importance, need to be acted upon in a different way. It is important to understand that when you move a message from one folder to the next in the process of deleting it, any attachments that came with the message also get moved and deleted. Whatever you do to the message, you automatically and simultaneously do to the attachments unless you take specific steps to obtain a different result.

When a message containing attachments is selected from your Inbox, the message itself is displayed in the message area provided within the template created by the email software program. In most cases the attachment (if it is a document) is not yet displayed there. Rather, there is a symbol showing you that the message contains an attachment. The software will give you two main options for what to do with the attachment. One option is to open the attachment. The other option is to save it. It is important to understand the difference between

choosing these two options. Consider the following example.

Let us say that you receive an email message that contains an attachment. The attachment is a document that has been produced by the sender using word processing software. Let us assume that your computer is equipped with the same software that was used by the sender to produce the document (which is generally a necessity in order to be able to open and use attachments). The attachment cannot be opened and viewed within the same template that displays the body of the email message, because it is produced using a different program.

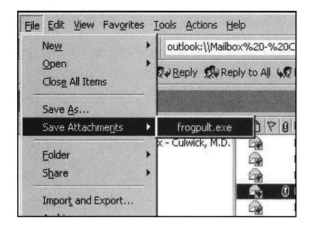

However, your operating system will recognize the program that was used to create the attached document. When you select the option for opening the attached document, your computer will first activate the program that was used to create it, if it is not already open, then the document will open within that program. When it does, it will have the exact same appearance as any document you may have created yourself using that same word processing software, and you will have the same range of options for working on the document as if it were one of your own — with one important exception. The document does not yet "exist" on your computer. In other words, it has not yet been saved in your computer's memory where you store your own documents. At the moment, the document only exists in the short term RAM memory of your computer (and back in your email program's Inbox where it was first received). After you take a look at the document, if you want to keep it indefinitely or permanently, you need to save it to one of the document folders on your computer's hard drive. We aren't going to detail the procedure for saving a document here. For the moment, we want you to understand why it is important to save the material. Once you have done so, you can close the file. This will return you to the email program that was running when you first viewed the message and elected to open the attachment. At this stage if you were to decide to delete the message from your email Inbox, and then also from your Deleted Items folder, the attachment would still exist on your hard drive, and you could go back and open it again at any time, work on it if need be, or send it to someone else at a later date. This is the significance of "saving" attachments.

We mentioned that when you click on an attachment you have two options: open or save. As we just described these options are not mutually exclusive in the sense that you can select open, and then go on to save the message in a separate step while it is displayed on your screen. However, perhaps you don't want to open the message at this time, you just want to save it for later. In this case you would select the save option. You would then be prompted to tell the computer where you want to save it. The main options are in a documents folder on your hard drive, or you can save it to a floppy disk or CD or DVD, depending on the external storage devices available on your computer.

Remember, however, that there is a difference between saving an attachment and saving the actual body of an email message. If you want to save the message itself and have it exist somewhere other than the Inbox of your email program, then as mentioned earlier you can use the Copy and Paste commands to create a version of the message within a word processing document (you can create a new document just to hold the message, or you can paste it into a document that already exists.) Unless you do this, the message will only exist within the email folder, and your options for what you can do with it there are limited unless or until you decide to make a copy of it elsewhere in your system.

Of course, there is an additional option for "saving" email messages and/or attachments, and that is to print them. While any message (or any attachment that you have opened) is displayed on your screen it is a simple procedure to activate the Print command. This will send the material to your printer to produce a paper copy. Sometimes keeping a message and/or attachment on paper in a file folder is the appropriate way to hold on to it for future reference. However, there are some disadvantages and limitations to this approach of which you need to be aware.

1) Printing a message from your Inbox is not the same as printing a document from your word processing program. For one thing, often the frame or "template" surrounding the message on the screen is printed along with the message itself. There are various ways to get around this constraint that you can learn, but be aware that the constraint may exist.

2) Printing is not an economical way to produce and store large volumes of material. There is the cost of the paper and ink, as well as the files needed to house the material. As more and more office communication is achieved by email, it is important to consider options for preserving these communications in one way or another. For example, a manager may want you to keep a file (either in paper or in your computer) of email correspondence that has gone back and forth between your department and a client, in case there should ever be a problem or dispute regarding instructions or details that were communicated. However, if printed records are not needed, creating them unnecessarily is not always a wise thing to do.

3) Paper files have two types of "security" problems. The first is the risk that someone without authorization will access them. The second is the risk that they may become lost or destroyed. If you print a message, then delete the message without copying or saving it, all you will ever have of that message is the paper version you printed.

In addition to saving, copying and/or printing incoming massages, the other main option you have is to send the message to someone else. This is called forwarding. If you receive a message that would be of interest to someone else in the company (or perhaps should have gone to them in the first place) then forwarding is a quick and easy way to deliver the message. It is important to realize that forwarding a message does not cause it to leave your own Inbox. You will still retain the message in your own system as well. Thus forwarding could perhaps be better described as "cloning". You make copies of the message to go to other people without losing your own copy.

When you select the Forward option, a template appears on your screen similar to what you would use to create a new message. However, the area where you would create a message is already filled with the current message that you intend to resend to someone else. Your email address appears automatically in the *From* field at the top of the template. All you need to do is insert the email address of the person to whom you wish to forward the message in the *To* field.

When forwarding a message you have the option of adding your own comments to the message. In most cases if you click at the beginning of the message an insertion point will appear and you can add your own comment. Some email programs allow you to forward a message that you have received as a separate attachment to a message that you originate. In this way you are able to keep your comments separate from the message you are forwarding.

Now that you know the basics of how to handle incoming email messages, we can turn our attention to creating them to send to others. There are two basic ways to start an email message to someone else. The first is by creating a brand new email message.

The software will guide you through the procedure for setting up the identifying "fields" for your message. These include your email address (which the program enters automatically), the email address of the receiver or receivers, and the name or title you wish to give to the message. It is very important to use the Title field for all business emails that you originate, and to give each message a good descriptive title that accurately but briefly describes the content of the message. The *title* field usually starts with the letters "*Re:*", which is the standard abbreviation that has traditionally been used to indicate the subject matter of a business letter.

There are also some optional fields you can use when creating a message. These are "*CC:*" and "*BCC:*". "*CC:*" is used to send a copy of the message to someone else. Again, this heading for the field makes use of a standard abbreviation that has traditionally been used in typed business letters (originally the "*CC*" stood for "carbon copy" back in the days when carbon paper was used to produce duplicate copies of letters as they were being typed). The designation *BCC* means "blind carbon copy". You use this field when you wish to send a copy to someone, but you do not want this person's name to appear in the version of the message that goes to the other parties. When you send the message simultaneously to more than one party,

all parties see all of the email names entered in the *To* and *CC* fields. However, they do not see any names entered into the *BCC* field.

It is important to understand when to use the *To*, *CC*, and *BCC* fields. Company policy is a factor, but in general if more than one party has equal need for the message, or involvement with its content, then these names go in the *To* field. If a person has a lesser involvement with the subject matter of the message, and is simply receiving a copy for general interest, then the name goes in the *CC* field. *BCC* is used if you do not want one or more parties named in the other fields to know that a copy is also being sent to a particular individual, or if that individual would not want their email address to become known to other parties receiving the message.

Whenever you need to place more than one email address in any of the *To, CC,* or *BCC* fields, you should type each email address, then insert a comma, then start the next name. As you will discover, there are alternatives to having to type the full email address each time you want to send a message. The email program has an address book in which you keep a record of the names of other parties with whom you frequently exchange email messages. You can select names from this directory and have them automatically

entered into the fields in your new message template, or when forwarding. Also, with many programs once you begin to type an email name that is already in the address book, the rest of the name will automatically appear, and you can accept it by clicking on it, or pressing the enter key.

Once you have set up the identifying information for your new outgoing email message, you click within the message box itself and begin typing your message. You can have different options for inputting and checking messages, as well as options for changing the appearance of your message, adding a signature, etc.

If you plan to send a message with an attachment, most people type the message first then perform the procedure to add the attachment. However, even after the attachment has been added, you always have the option of returning to the message to make additional changes.

The first step in adding an attachment is to click on the appropriate button on your software template. Then, depending on the program, you will be prompted to

identify where the attachment will be found, and then to select the specific file you wish to attach. In most cases the source will be a folder somewhere on your hard drive, although you can also take an attachment from a floppy disc or a CD or DVD. Attachments can be word-processed text files, pictures, or multimedia files of various types.

Once your message is carefully checked and ready to go, the last step is to click the Send button. Realize that you cannot get a message back after it has been successfully sent, so be sure everything is perfect before you perform this final step. If you are not sure you can always save the message as a Draft and then go back and take another look at it later before sending it.

We mentioned earlier that there are two ways of starting a message you wish to send to someone else. What we have described up to now is the first and main method, which is to originate a new message yourself on your computer. However, there is a second method, which is to reply to a message you have received from someone else.

There are two situations in which email users tend to use the Reply button. The first is to provide a specific answer to a specific incoming message. When you select Reply, a message template opens up for you. All of the identifying fields are already filled in.

The *To* field will show the email name of the person who sent you the message. The *From* field will show your email name. The *Re* (Title) field will show the title that the original sender gave to the message, unless you click in this field and type a new title. With all these fields already completed, all you have to do is begin typing your reply, then press Send when you are sure it is as you want it to be.

There is a second possible use of the Reply function, but it is one that is not generally recommended for business emails. Sometimes email users wish to take a "shortcut" when creating a new message. Instead of having to fill in the identifying fields from scratch, if they go into an old message received from the party and select Reply, a message template will open up already addressed to that party. This saves a couple of steps. However, it can also

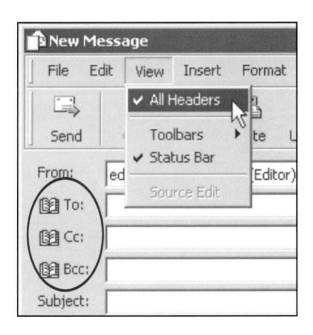

create confusion. Unless you change it (and people doing this to save time seldom bother) the title of your message will be the same title as that of the old message. This may have nothing at all to do with the content of the new message you wish to send. For people who are emailing their personal friends on a casual basis, message titles often aren't particularly important. However, in a professional message you should be sure that all of your messages carry an appropriate title. As a general rule, only use the reply function when you are actually replying to the content of someone else's message. Whenever you want to send a message on a new or different subject, start a new message and title it appropriately.

There is another factor of which you should be aware when replying to business messages. Many business messages are addressed to more than one party. In email programs there are generally two reply options: Reply and Reply to All. If you select Reply to All your reply will be sent not only to the party who sent you the message, but to others who are named as co-receivers of that message. This feature is occasionally convenient when several parties are participating in a group discussion on a topic, but it has created embarrassment for email users on many occasions. Sometimes you have a response that is only intended for one person in particular. If you accidentally hit Reply to All, however, it will be seen by other people as well. Therefore, it is important to watch carefully which reply button you select (and it is also a good idea to use discretion in the wording of any message so as not to run a needless risk of offending some other colleague). Even if you send the reply only to one person, there is nothing stopping that person from forwarding it to others. A disadvantage of email is that it is so quick and easy to use that it lends itself to impulse and indiscretion. Remember: once you have sent an email message, you cannot reverse the action, nor can you control what other people choose to do with your messages.

We mentioned earlier that you can keep an address book of your regular email contacts. This both preserves important information on how to contact people, as well as facilitates a more rapid addressing of outgoing messages. In the address book you will generally enter the person's actual name as well as their email address. Depending on how your system is set up, your incoming and outgoing messages may display the real names of correspondents. However, you must have an actual email address stored in your system in order to send a message. There are various types of online directories that can be used to help find another party's email address. You can generally find out how to contact business parties by visiting their company's website. Most websites have a "contact us" option that allows you to send email messages to the company. There are two basic ways in which these contact options tend to be set up. With one option clicking on a highlighted link will cause your computer to open up your own email program and email creation template, with the company's name already entered into the To field. This is generally the most desirable way to send a message, because you end up retaining a copy of the message in your Sent folder.

However, some companies manage their "Contact Us" feature in a different way. Instead of a link that opens up a conventional email message to a specified address, they present you with a questionnaire that you must complete, giving your own contact information, then allowing you to type in a specific question or message, often of limited length, in a text box provided. The disadvantage of this form of contact is that you don't end up learning the company's email address, nor do you have a copy of your message saved in your own email files. However, if this is the only option presented to you, sometimes you can use it to send a short message requesting the email address of a specific party or department with whom you wish to correspond. You may then receive a reply with the necessary address.

As we stated earlier, many people get into the habit of allowing a great many incoming and outgoing email messages to accumulate in their system folders. Besides wasting storage space, this can make it very difficult to go back and locate a specific message at a later date, especially if significant time has passed and a lot of other messages have accumulated in the meantime. For this reason most email programs offer a "Find" feature that allows you to locate an old stored message without having to search through them all at random. Any "find" operation on a computer makes use of what is called a "search string". This is specific, word-for-word information that you know is contained within the message for which you are searching. The string may relate to the title of the message, the name of the sender, some key phrase within the message, or a combination of elements. The more specific the search string the more precisely the software will locate what you are looking for. The Find template will encourage you to fill in as many

details about the "lost" message as you can remember, so it can narrow down the field as much as possible. If all you know is the name of the sender, and you have many messages from the same sender, the software will end up finding many items that meet this simple criterion. However, if you can make the search criteria more specific, the possibilities can be narrowed down. Search strings usually need to be literally correct, letter-for-letter. If you search for a title or phrase you seem to remember that turns out to be slightly different from the actual phrase that was used in the message, the software may not find what you are looking for. The computer will display the headings of as many messages as it can find that match the criteria you have specified. One way you can narrow the search is to use the "Received before" or "Received after" fields. If you know approximately when the message was originally sent to you, you can select to disregard anything before and/or after the dates that bracket your approximate recollection of the date the message was received. This may greatly pare down the possibilities to a small enough number of entries that you can open them individually until you find the one you wanted. There are other types of search criteria you can use to narrow the field in cases where you can't remember the precise title of the message. For example you can check off an option that instructs the software to look for messages with or without attachments.

There is one other option we should mention with regard to organizing email messages, one that can help reduce the need to undertake complex searches of old messages, or the risk of losing track of material of which you may have some ongoing need. Earlier we described the basic types of folders that are automatically provided under Outlook Express or other similar email programs. However, many computer operators don't realize that there is the option of creating and naming new folders. Messages will not be delivered to these new folders. However, after reading a message in the Inbox the user has the option of moving it to a separate folder. By using one or more special folders in this way, messages that need to be saved for a later date can be segregated from the messages that tend to accumulate in the Inbox and Sent Items folders. Messages from either or both of these folders can be moved to new folders. Because these email folders do not treat messages as individual documents, there is still some limitation to the security of any message or attachment that is being saved only within the email system. Saving attachments to document folders on the hard drive and copying and pasting the content of messages into text documents are still better

options for obtaining copies of key material for long term use, and possible reworking at a later date.

Anticipating and Managing Email Problems

Email is revolutionizing business communications. However, like any revolution it is not without its problems. Earlier in this text we alluded to some of them: time wasted sending and receiving unnecessary messages or messages that are not work-related, inappropriate distribution of messages to parties who have no need to see them, security risks due to information falling into the wrong hands, or indiscrete messages being composed without sufficient care and forethought. The fact that email is so easy to use is part of the problem. Too many business people get caught in the heat of the moment where they email first and think later.

However, there are other problems inherent in the system other than careless or indiscrete use. One problem is that a small but significant number of email messages never reach their destination for a variety of reasons. If there is an error in the message address making it undeliverable, in many cases the sender will eventually be notified of this fact. Email service providers have programs called daemons that report back to users on many, but not all, of their undeliverable messages. A message will be undeliverable if an error is made in inputting the receiver's email address. Even the slightest error, such as a single missing or misplaced letter or punctuation mark, will make the message undeliverable. Unlike the postal service, which often tries to deliver mail that contains a slight but decipherable error in the address, email services do not correct misspelled addresses or guess at possible destinations.

An address error is not the only possible cause of a delivery failure. Other possible causes include the receiver's email box exceeding the allowable storage space, or problems with the equipment or programs somewhere along the delivery path. The daemon will return the message along with a rather technical report detailing

the reason for the failure and the attempts that were made to complete the delivery. If the failure was caused by a mistake in inputting the address, you can send the message again with the correct data. However, some of the other causes for failure may be conditions you can do nothing about, other than wait and try again later, hoping for a better result.

Unfortunately on occasion the system failure is, at least in part, the daemon itself and it fails to report on the failed delivery. The problem here is that the sender ends up with no idea that a failure has occurred. Because email generally proceeds smoothly, we have a tendency to assume our messages get through and are seen by the receiver unless we hear otherwise. When this doesn't happen, we tend to get caught off guard. You may be sitting at your desk for hours or even days wondering why the other party is ignoring you and failing to respond to some urgent message when the simple fact may be that the party never received it. You should always keep this possibility in the back of your mind when you do not receive an expected reply to a message. Before jumping to conclusions, particularly in the case of a colleague or business associate who normally responds promptly, it is often worth sending a second message politely inquiring as to whether the person received the first one.

Messages can be lost due to unusual problems in the system, or a mistake made by the receiver. The receiver may accidentally delete a message before reading it, or it can end up buried in among other messages that have already been read, causing the receiver not to notice it. However, another frequent cause of "lost messages" is the growing use of Spam filters. The term "spam" refers to unsolicited and unwanted email messages, often sent out in bulk to large numbers of email addresses, frequently trying to sell some company's product or service. There are so many spam emails being sent that they can hinder the ability to notice and reply to legitimate messages from people you actually know or do business with. To reduce the hassles of dealing with large amounts of spam, many email programs and/or service providers now offer "spam filters". These filters, in principle, detect messages that are sent out in bulk and route them to a special box, keeping them separate from your "real" messages and allowing you to ignore or delete them. The problem is that these filters don't always work as well as one would like, and sometimes legitimate messages, especially those that come from a corporate email address, are accidentally and incorrectly dumped into the spam mail box. For this reason if you have such a box set up on your system it is important to check it from time to time and not delete the contents indiscriminately without taking a quick look at the names of the parties that have sent you messages. Spam filters generally come with some sort of "This is not spam" option. If you find a message in the spam mail box that doesn't belong there (i.e. a legitimate message from someone you know or with whom you wish to do business) then you can click on this option. This instructs the filter not to direct future messages from the sender into the spam mail box.

The other significant problem with email is that unfortunately it is a major conduit for computer viruses. In brief, a computer virus is a malicious and destructive computer program that is attached to a website, file, or message, and invades and harms the computer system of anyone who opens it. Viruses represent criminal acts, and it is hard to fathom the motivation of their perpetrators, since viruses often spread at random, harming people with whom their creators have no knowledge or association, and from which they derive no financial benefit as a result of the attack. These malicious programs are called "viruses" because they are designed to be self-replicating. When a virus affects your computer it is often programmed to find your email address book and send out copies of the virus to all the contacts you have stored there.

No one would ever open an email message containing a computer virus if

they realized what it was. Viruses cleverly disguise themselves as routine email messages. When they get into a person's address book they send themselves out disguised as messages from that person. In other words, if you get an email virus on your computer it may send messages to your colleagues that appear to come from you, and you may have no idea that the virus is doing this until it is too late to stop it.

We are mentioning computer viruses in this section because email attachments, while not the only method, are one of the most common methods by which viruses are spread. It is difficult, though not impossible, to embed the complex coding needed to generate a virus within the body of a text message. However, email attachments afford the perfect opportunity for doing this. You might think that the attachment you are

receiving is a document, photo, or some other type of file, when it may actually be a virus. Without anti-virus protection once it is opened on your computer it is very difficult to stop the consequences or remove the virus from your computer without professional assistance. Sometimes viruses can cause permanent and irreparable damage to computer programs and files.

The first line of protection against email-borne viruses is an effective and up-to-date anti-virus software package installed on your computer. With regard to a company-owned computer it is generally the employer's responsibility to select and support the software you will be using. In any large company there will likely be a computer specialist on staff who will assist with issues such as virus protection. Once installed, anti-virus software screens email automatically without any specific action on your part. However the software needs to be updated frequently (some programs update daily) in order for the program to keep up with the latest viruses that are circulating.

Unfortunately the cleverest (and most dangerous) viruses sometimes defeat the anti-virus software, or a computer is infected before the software is updated to the latest threat. You should be suspicious of certain types of email messages and avoid opening them — or at least avoid opening the attachments that are sent with them. As a general rule you should hesitate to open an email attachment from anyone whose email address you do not recognize, or where the title of the message is unusually vague. Of course, sometimes this is difficult to do if the nature of your job requires you to communicate by email with the general public and receiving messages from unknown sources is routine. However, you need to consider whether a specific incoming message fits the expected pattern of such correspondence. Because email viruses replicate themselves on many different computers and are re-sent unknowingly by many people in many situations, they tend to have very vague titles such as "Your invoice" or "Your Inquiry". A message that mentions some specific project you are working on or service your company provides is unlikely to contain a virus (remember: virus criminals don't usually design their messages with a specific target in mind). If you don't recognize the sender's name, the title of the message seems vague, and you cannot think of a good reason why someone would be sending you an attachment, then be suspicious of it. You can get someone with greater expertise in this area to look at the message for you. You can send a message to the sender asking whether or not they in fact sent you the message. (Remember that the "sender"

of the infected message is not the creator of the virus, but rather some previous victim who probably doesn't yet know that his computer has a virus.) If the original message did contain a virus, chances are you won't receive a reply, whereas if it was a legitimate message the party will likely reply to you and explain what was sent. Unless the explanation is satisfactory, don't open any attachment that comes with the second message either.

Viruses keep finding new and ever more devious ways to disguise themselves and trick recipients into opening them. Some come as implausible announcements saying that you've won a contest you never entered. Some even come disguised as an email daemon that is returning an undeliverable message to you. Unless such a message is very specific and makes reference in the body of the message to an actual email that you did in fact send out, never open the attachment that comes with such a message. Another way that people open themselves up to viruses is by forwarding jokes or gags. Most of these are harmless, but some contain viruses — and all are a waste of valuable office time. Be suspicious of these, especially when they come from someone you do not know. To some extent, like real biological viruses, your risk of getting a computer virus also increases in proportion to your association with people who are more likely to be "sick". For example, pornography sites on the Internet are frequent sources of viruses and spyware. Not all viruses cripple the receiver's computer, and some can lurk there for a while, attaching themselves to various types of files, and then being transmitted if copies of the files are sent to other people.

Let's put it this way. Imagine that your office computer is infected with a virus, and perhaps spreads across an internal network to other employees.

Eventually the source of the virus will be tracked down to your computer and some specific operation you performed. Whether or not you will be blamed for launching the virus depends on what you were doing at the time. If it came attached to or disguised as a business communication or document that you would have had little reason to be suspicious of, there is no reason for you to be blamed. However if it was launched as a result of some joke, or a visit to a disreputable Internet site, or a very obvious "phony" message that you should have recognized, at the very least you will feel embarrassed, and your reputation at the company may suffer. We want to make you aware of the significance to the management of your routine office communications.

Sending and Receiving Faxes

The single-function fax machine is slowly on its way out. To begin with, the fax process has been incorporated into work centers that also perform other functions. More importantly, however, these days there are better and cheaper methods of sending most types of documents. Having said that, it will be a while yet before the technology disappears entirely, so all administrative assistants need to know the basics of how to manage fax operations.

Some companies still send documents of many different types either among themselves or to other organizations via the conventional fax machine. Even those companies that largely use email attachments for most documents still find the fax machine useful for certain purposes. For example, if a person quickly needs to receive a copy of a signed document, faxes are often used. It would be possible to scan the original document and then transmit it as an email attachment, but not everyone has this technical capability yet. It should be noted that copies of documents received by fax may be limited in terms of satisfying legal requirements, since the transmission quality of the fax may not allow the validity of a signature or notation to be verified. However, for many business purposes a reasonably good quality fax is "sufficient" to initiate various types of procedures. We won't spend a great

deal of time on this technology, but it is certainly worthy of mention.

One traditional problem with sending paper faxes is making sure that they are given to the right party within an organization. Individual workers don't often tend to have personal fax machines at their desks. Rather there is usually one machine for the entire department. One reason for this is that a fax machine needs to be attached to a telephone line that is set up for fax transmissions. Some phone lines can be switched back and forth between fax and voice telephone use. However, most businesses, and certainly all who tend to send and receive a large volume of fax transmissions, tend to purchase a dedicated phone line and phone number for this purpose. There is some cost involved in these extra lines, and it is not feasible to have a great number scattered around an office.

The result is that incoming faxes often need to be distributed to various parties. In order to facilitate this process, it has become traditional for a fax transmission to be preceded by a single cover sheet. The cover sheet is like a "title page". It identifies specifically the sender and receiver. The other very important piece of information that should be contained on the cover sheet is the number of pages transmitted. Often a document is taken off the fax machine too quickly, before the transmission is finished, or a final page may accidentally be gathered with another fax that came through just behind it. Identifying the number of pages in the transmission helps prevent this from happening. A numbering system is used to further aid in keeping the transmission together. If a transmission includes 4 pages, then the first page is marked 1/4 (meaning the first of four). Subsequent pages are marked 2/4, 3/4, and 4/4.

Some people put the date and time on fax cover sheets. However, this is not always necessary, because most fax machines print a "header line" at the top of each page of the fax. This line generally shows the date and time, the phone number from which the fax was transmitted, and in some cases the name of the sender. If your fax machine is set to transmit a header line it is important to ensure that it is programmed to give accurate and up-to-date information. For example, if the date is not set correctly on the machine then an incorrect date will be printed in the header.

The procedural details of how to use a fax machine vary with make and model. The operations are fairly simple, and you will learn them quickly on the job. Generally you have to place the outgoing pages in the correct tray, then key in the fax number of the destination and press a Send button. Most fax machines scan the entire transmission

first before it is sent. The machine will then "eject" the pages once the scanning is complete. This doesn't mean that the transmission is finished, however. The machine may hold the material in memory for some time while waiting for a chance to complete the transmission successfully. For this reason many machines are programmed to print a transmission report once the fax is completed. Fax machines are programmed to communicate with one another and verify whether the other machine has received a transmission successfully. The transmission report will tell you whether the communication went through successfully, or if there was a problem. It will also confirm the number of pages that were successfully transmitted. You should verify that this number corresponds with what you intended to include in the transmission.

Many fax machines have a built-in call back function. You can program the machine to make a specified number of additional tries if the transmission cannot go through the first time — usually because the receiver's line is busy. It is very important that you use extreme care when inputting numbers into a fax machine. If you make a mistake the machine will try to send your material to the wrong number. If the incorrect number happens to be connected to someone else's fax machine then your potentially confidential documents will be sent to someone who has no business seeing it. However, just as bad, if the incorrect number you keyed in is not connected to a fax machine, but to someone's regular phone number, then your fax machine may dial this number over and over unsuccessfully trying to transmit each time, which annoys and harasses some innocent member of the public. Unfortunately fax machines have no way of knowing that you entered a wrong number. If programmed to try 20 times to send the message, it will phone someone's number 20 times, and there will be little the person can do to make the harassing phone calls stop until the fax machine reaches the maximum number of tries. Besides taking care when keying in the number in the first place, it is a good idea not to wander too far away from the fax machine until you are sure your transmission has gone through. If you see that the machine

is making repeated unsuccessful tries, you should double-check that you have entered the correct number.

In the past many organizations transmitted faxes at night when phone rates were lower. This is no longer as common a practice, in part because faxes themselves are becoming less common, but also because many modern long distance plans don't charge higher rates for daytime calls. However, some organizations — especially those that have worldwide dealings — leave their fax machines plugged in and turned on 24 hours a day. If you ever work in such a situation, before leaving the office it is important to ensure that the machine has enough paper and toner to print any faxes that may be received after hours.

One impediment to leaving fax machines turned on all the time is the problem of "junk faxes". These are advertisements indiscriminately sent to a great many fax numbers by various businesses. What adds insult to injury with these advertisements is that the receiver ends up paying for them in the costs of paper, toner, wear and tear on the machine, and staff time needed to weed through and dispose of them. Fortunately the era of the junk fax is now fading with the fax machine itself (having been replaced by the era of spam - the junk email).

Processing Incoming and Outgoing Mail

As an administrative assistant or departmental secretary it may be your responsibility to process incoming and outgoing mail — not only mail addressed to yourself, but also to your manager and perhaps to others within the department. In this section we will look simultaneously at mail sent via the government postal service, as well as items shipped by private couriers. It is particularly important to have an efficient system for performing this task for several reasons:

• Many companies incur considerable costs in mail and shipping. Each item has a particular postal or courier cost associated with it, above and beyond the cost in staff time to process it.

• Items that arrive in the mail are sometimes unique and irreplaceable, or at least not easily replaced. In addition to correspondence and paper documents, many types of tangible items are also shipped in this way.

• An incoming piece of mail can easily become lost or misdirected because, obviously, it exists in a unique place and time, unlike an electronic communication that can be duplicated and retransmitted. A lost or stolen piece of mail is often gone forever. Even if the shipment is merely a document with no monetary value, it is impossible to predict the harm that could come to the company as a result of mishandling. In an extreme case it could result in a lost order or even a lost client.

- Items sent in the mail are easier for unauthorized people to intercept and steal than electronic communications. Theft from the mail, either internal or external, is a serious problem in some organizations, and it is at least a passing concern in most others.

The details of mail handling procedures vary from one organization to another. A key variable is whether or not the company is large enough, or does enough volume of mail transactions, to have a separate shipping department that handles mail for the company. If it does, then much of the work of preparing outgoing mail may lie with this department. It may pick up items from other departments and look after affixing postage or calling couriers. However, even if this task is partially handled by another department, there will generally be strict rules as to how outgoing mail is to be prepared by administrative assistants. You will likely be responsible not only for addressing the outgoing items, but perhaps also for their packaging. In the case of items going by courier, you may be expected to prepare "waybills" that record the details of the shipment. A waybill is like a multi-copy address label that also contains account and billing information. A portion of the waybill is detached and affixed to the parcel as a label. Waybills contain barcodes that allow courier shipments to be scanned when they are picked up by the courier,

when they are successfully delivered, and at various points along the way. This allows for on-line tracking of parcels, as well as tracing any that go astray or are unexpectedly delayed.

The post office and private couriers also have their own rules for what may or may not be shipped, how it should be labeled, and the type of container or packaging that is required. Most parcels sent via the post office are charged by weight. Weight is also a factor in courier charges. However, many couriers offer a flat rate for any shipment that will fit within a standard sized envelope or package supplied by the courier company. If you regularly ship materials by courier to a particular destination it is important to be aware of how the courier company assesses charges, and look for ways to save money by combining items or by selecting a more economical packaging option.

Besides weight, the other significant cost factor in sending items by mail or courier is the level of service desired. Your company may have strict policies regarding the speed and urgency, and consequent cost level, of shipments. However, in some cases it may be up to you to select the level of service for a specific item, either by yourself or in consultation with your manager. A common source of wasted money in many companies is the overuse of courier service in general, and overnight courier service in particular, for documents or materials that are not really that urgent. Sending a simple document by regular mail will still cost less than a dollar to most North American destinations, and it will arrive within a few days. Sending the same material by courier could cost $10 or more, even when the company receives a volume discount from the courier company. Sending parcels by overnight courier can be considerably more expensive than that. To make their service more competitive with the post office, many couriers now offer the option of air or ground delivery. Air delivery is generally next day, whereas ground service may take two or three days to most North American destinations. A considerable savings can be had by allowing the extra day or two, especially when the company ships a large volume of material.

On the other hand, there are times when rush delivery is essential. Some courier services offer different levels of air service. For example, there may be a slightly different rate for 9:00 a.m. delivery the next morning, or afternoon

delivery later that day. Some couriers offer same day delivery under some circumstances. The faster you want the item to be guaranteed for delivery, the costlier the service.

We are describing postal and courier services as though they are two separate options. However, you should be aware that both the U.S. and Canadian government postal services now offer their own version of courier service. They also offer a broad range of special services associated with the "regular" postal system, such as guaranteed two- or three- day delivery for a price that falls between the overnight courier service and that of regular mail delivery. Special services also include insurance, special delivery, and confirmation delivery cards that are returned to the sender when a delivery has been successfully completed.

Speed is not the only reason to consider using these special services. Another significant benefit of courier service, or special postal services is that, unlike regular mail, they offer the ability to track a shipment. This provides greater security, since items that are sent in a tracked system are somewhat less likely to be stolen than those deposited into the regular mail chutes. If you mail a letter or parcel by regular mail and it doesn't arrive at its destination when expected, you have no way to find out where it is or what may have happened to it. You can purchase insurance on parcels that will allow you to recover the value of an item that goes astray, but sometimes compensation isn't the main issue. When an important item fails to be delivered it can cause other problems for the company that sends it, depending on the nature and purpose of the shipment. Even when next day delivery is not essential, many businesses purchase a higher level of service than the regular postal option in order to

reduce the risk of their shipments being lost and stolen, and in order to obtain and preserve proof of successful delivery. When items are sent via regular (uninsured and untracked) mail, not only is there the risk that a postal employee or someone else along the way will intercept the delivery and steal the item, there may also be the risk that an unscrupulous customer will actually receive the item but then claim not to have done so.

These days computerization has permeated the postal and courier businesses as it has virtually everything else. A lot of very useful tasks can now be accomplished online by visiting the websites of the post office and/or the courier company with which your company does business. You can find addresses and ZIP or postal codes. You can identify levels of service, and learn the rates for a specific service to a specific destination. You can download and print address labels and other paperwork. You can even summon a courier to come and make a pickup. Naturally, if your company has a shipping department they may handle some of these tasks, but you should know about them as well.

If your company does a large volume of postage and/or courier shipping, then trucks may arrive automatically at fixed times each business day for pick-ups. The shipping department may post

the times by which they need to receive items from you in order to make them ready for a specified pick-up. It is important for you to be aware of these times. Suppose right before lunch your manager gives you an item that must be sent by overnight courier. Let us say that the policy of your shipping department is that it needs to receive courier items packaged and ready to go by 3:00 p.m. in order to make a 3:30 scheduled pick-up by the courier truck. Somehow you get distracted and don't get the material together and over to shipping until just after that deadline. Your tardiness could mean the difference between the material being on the client's desk bright and early the next morning, or not arriving until the following day.

When it comes to international shipments there is some additional information you need to know and consider when preparing outgoing mail or courier shipments. In addition to international postal rates you also need to be aware of Customs duties and restrictions in the country that will be receiving the shipment. There are some items you are not allowed to ship internationally, or to specific countries, and if you ship anything other than routine business documents you must be aware of any restrictions that may apply. Many countries also charge duties on shipments of merchandise imported from other countries and some also charge a sales tax. Payment of duties is the responsibility of the receiver. However, by being aware of the situation the receiver will face, you can take various steps to ensure that the receiver is not unduly inconvenienced. Proper labeling of international shipments is essential, and they must be labeled using the correct customs forms. In most cases you can obtain customs forms from the post office in your own country that will be acceptable to customs officials at the destination country. Sometimes, however, a different form is required depending on the nature or weight of the shipment, and depending on the class of delivery service. Items must be described accurately and their financial value, if any, must be stated. Most forms also require you to indicate the net weight of each item. The term "net weight" refers to the weight excluding any packaging materials. Some customs forms also require you to indicate what you would like to have done with the material if it should prove to be undeliverable for any reason. If you want it returned to you in such a case, you may have to agree to pay the costs of that return shipment.

Up to now we have described typical tasks and considerations for the processing of outgoing mail and courier shipments. However, as an administrative assistant you can also be responsible for sorting, opening, and distributing incoming items addressed not only to yourself, but also to your manager, other staff members, or the department in general. Sometimes an administrative assistant or departmental secretary is asked to open all incoming mail for the department, regardless of whom it is addressed to, unless a particular item is marked "personal and confidential". There are a couple of reasons for this practice, since in private life you are not accustomed to opening envelopes addressed to other people. To begin with, mail addressed to a business address is generally considered to be the property of the company, and not the employee whose name appears on it. The assumption is that the person is not being contacted personally, but rather in the capacity of a corporate figure. In your capacity as another corporate figure it is appropriate for you to provide whatever assistance the company deems necessary in responding to the incoming correspondence. If the company wishes you to handle a particular task, rather than have it handled by the person whose name is

indicated (perhaps incorrectly), it is within the company's rights to do so.

You may sometimes even find that you are asked to open mail that has come in for an employee who no longer works for the company. Again, unless it is marked as a personal and confidential item, the presumption is that the sender's intention was to communicate with the company. From a company's point of view employees are often interchangeable, and it is perfectly acceptable to assign a task from one employee to another.

On a practical level it often happens that people outside of the company don't really understand how their correspondence should be addressed, and a large percentage is actually misdirected — sometimes sent to the wrong person within a department, in other cases sent to the wrong department altogether. Thus, the first and primary purpose of an administrative assistant when opening mail is to detect any such problems and immediately redirect the item appropriately. In essence, the aim is better customer service by ensuring that all mail is directed properly and acted upon in a timely fashion. Needless to say, you cannot perform this basic function unless or until you have acquired a thorough understanding of the company's business and which staff members handle which tasks.

Another reason for opening all departmental mail is to ensure that priority items are acted upon right away. Depending on the nature of the business you may be asked to segregate payments, applications, contracts, complaints, or other specific items and highlight them for immediate action. In some cases you may be trained and authorized to undertake this action yourself. In other cases your task will simply be to bring the item to the attention of the staff member who has been assigned to handle it.

Not all companies ask administrative assistants to handle incoming mail in this way. Some companies take a very different approach, and do not permit staff members to open mail that is addressed specifically to someone else.

However, the same problem will arise in that a certain percentage of mail will have been mislabeled or misdirected by the senders. Consequently, after the mail has been opened by the original addressees, some of it may return to your desk to be redistributed or acted upon. Either system can work. What matters is that you understand both the procedural specifics and the general rationale behind the system in place, and follow it consistently and effectively.

Some managers will ask you to sort and prioritize their incoming mail. When there is a large volume of daily mail, this saves the manager valuable time and ensures that important items don't get lost in the pile. Again, it is important that you take note of your manager's instructions and preferences and set up a clear, consistent, and comfortable interaction that satisfies the manager's needs and wishes in this regard. The specific system used to label or flag particular items is less important than the fact that both parties understand the system, are comfortable with it, and it achieves their needs in as efficient a manner as possible.

Disposal of Communications

Unfortunately, disposal of communications is becoming an increasingly important topic. Not that long ago expressions such as "industrial espionage" and "identity theft" were all but unheard of. However, these days there is a growing problem with unscrupulous individuals obtaining access to both electronic and paper communications and materials and using confidential information they obtain to harm organizations, employees, and/or customers. At the level of industrial espionage it is generally unscrupulous competitors who try to steal and profit from client information or trade secrets. On the other hand, identity theft is more a problem faced by individual consumers. It occurs when a criminal gains access to confidential information such as credit card or bank account numbers, as well as other information needed to access them. You might assume that the burden of preventing identity theft would lie primarily with credit card companies, banks, and consumers themselves. However, frequently a weak link in the chain of protection is companies that do not adequately protect information about their customers. Many companies gain critical information about individuals in the course of doing business with them. This information includes credit card numbers and expiry dates, signatures, and sometimes even vital statistics such as date of birth, bank account information, or other information that could be used by criminals to steal from these individuals or harm them in some other way.

Companies fail to adequately protect information by:

1) failing to establish and enforce adequate safeguards on websites that collect sensitive information

2) failing to dispose properly of paper records and duplicate copies of sensitive materials

3) failing to use adequate care to verify numbers and authorizations when faxing or emailing sensitive information

4) using non-secure communications methods, such as cell phones, when discussing sensitive subjects.

As an administrative assistant it is usually not your role to set corporate policy with regard to use of websites and email, paper shredders, or cell phones. However, it is your responsibility to understand, obey, and help implement and enforce those policies, and to help ensure that others around you appreciate their significance.

You should be aware of security issues on a day-to-day basis. This awareness includes a wide range of practices and concerns, such as:

- attention to what is on your desk and within sight of persons who may approach your desk, especially if you will be away from your desk

- similar awareness to what is visible on your computer monitor

- ensuring that mail is distributed correctly within the department

- ensuring that discarded communications and documents are shredded and disposed of securely

- ensuring that stored email messages are properly safeguarded with passwords and that messages are deleted properly when no longer needed

- maintaining security features when using the voice mail system

- protecting any and all passwords related to communications, and taking care to prevent others from discovering or guessing the passwords you have selected

- avoiding unnecessary duplication and distribution of electronic or paper communications

- taking care that documents are not accidentally left behind in the photocopy machine, fax machine, or work center

- ensuring that paper filing cabinets are locked and that security procedures for access to them are followed at all times

At one time people communicated mainly or exclusively through face-to-face conversations. Only those present and within earshot at a particular moment in time gained information from such communications, and once they were over there was no record that they ever happened. As we have evolved we have found newer and better ways of communicating. We have also discovered that it can be very handy to have records of our own communications so that the information can be preserved. In a perfect world, this would be great. However, in the world we live in the communication records we keep and distribute can, and often do, come back to haunt us, because they can broaden the circle of participants in these communications to include individuals we never intended. With the privilege of being able to preserve records of our communications comes the responsibility of protecting those records.

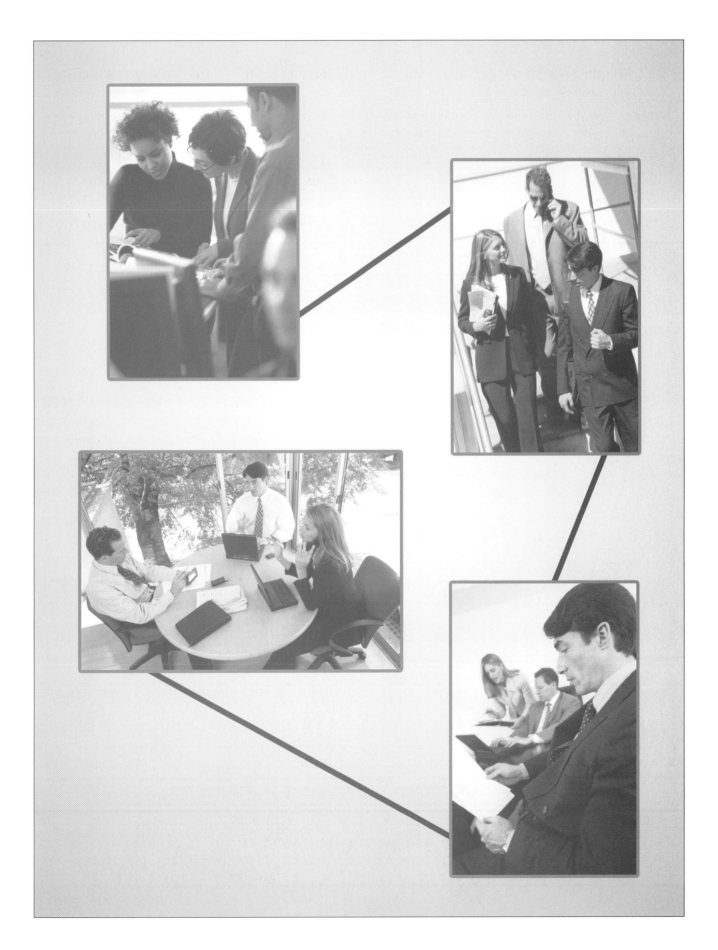

Chapter 3

ARRANGING AND ASSISTING
with Meetings and Conferences

Types of Meetings and Meeting-Related Tasks

As an administrative assistant one of your important duties will be to help your manager with meetings of various types. Almost any business situation involves meetings of one type or another, and in some offices arranging meetings is a primary administrative function. The types of meetings that will be conducted vary according to the nature of the company's work, but may include any or all of the following:

1) regularly scheduled internal staff meetings

2) ad hoc staff meetings called to discuss a particular project, problem, or issue

3) meetings called by senior management to disseminate important information to the work force

4) internal meetings or seminars that are based on training or professional development

5) external meetings or conferences for training or professional development

6) sales force meetings

7) project-related meetings with a client group

8) attending and participating in trade shows

Regardless of the purpose of the meeting or the subject matter being discussed, the duties of the administrative assistant are determined more by the fundamental logistical nature of the meeting. From this perspective there are three main "generic types" of meetings:

1) meetings where participants physically assemble in your manager's office or in a conference facility within your department

2) "virtual meetings" that will be conducted from your office or facility, but where some of the participants will be participating from a distance via audio or audio/video technology

3) meetings that will be conducted at a rented facility either within your own city or a distant location.

Again viewing this area from the perspective of the tasks assigned to an administrative assistant, there is one other way to classify meetings:

1) meetings your manager will attend alone, and be merely an attendee, not a leader

2) meetings you will be attending with your manager, but neither of you will be expected to play a leading role

3) meetings that your manager will organize and lead, with your assistance, and where afterwards you will be responsible for preparing a written report of what transpired

4) meetings that your manager will lead or help lead, but no direct assistance or participation is needed from you once the meeting starts or afterwards.

The reason we are sorting meetings out in this last set of categories is because it prepares us to look at specific tasks that an administrative assistant might be asked to perform related to a meeting. As you will see from the following list, some of these tasks center around "geography" (where the meeting is taking place), while others center on "technology" (what your manager's role and actions will be during the meeting, and what assistance you will be expected to provide).

- making travel and accommodation arrangements (a topic we will discuss in more detail later in this text)

- preparing and distributing invitations/announcements concerning the meeting

- preparing written and/or multi-media materials and presentations to be used during the meeting and setting up any equipment that will be needed

- taking notes during the meeting and then writing "minutes" or some other written summation and report of what took place.

There is another possible activity worth a quick mention. If your manager will be giving a speech at a conference, you may be asked to help with preparation of the speech, inputting and editing, and/or transferring all or part of the speech onto cue cards. However, this is a more specialized task and one that only a relatively small percentage of administrative assistants will become involved with.

Invitations or Announcements for Meetings

As an administrative assistant it may be your responsibility to inform participants of a meeting that is being organized by your manager. The manner in which you convey this information will depend on whether the meeting involves employees or persons outside of the company, whether the meeting is formal or informal, and whether or not detailed instructions or preparations for the meeting must be conveyed.

The simplest way to invite participants to attend a less formal meeting is by phone call, especially when the participants are all members of the local office staff. However, there are several disadvantages to this approach, including the following:

• If there are several people who need to be informed and invited, then making the phone calls can be time consuming. If some explanation of the purpose of the meeting must be given, explaining this to each person individually can be repetitive. If some participants are difficult to reach by phone and you need to leave voice mail messages you may need to follow up to ensure that the message was received in time, especially if short notice is given.

• If there is anything controversial about the nature of the meeting, or if the subject matter is complex, you may be drawn into providing explanations that are best left for your manager to make during the meeting itself.

• You do not have a record of the information you conveyed to the participants during the phone call.

Perhaps the only advantage to the telephone call method is that in the case of each participant whom you are able to reach personally, they will have no excuse for failing to show up. They won't be able to claim they didn't get the message.

In many situations a more efficient method of notifying/inviting participants is to send an email message. This approach offers the following advantages:

• One message can be addressed to many different parties simultaneously. If there is a group of people who always attend these meetings you can set up a group of addresses in your address book, then select the group in the *To* field of your message.

• Email allows you to convey more precise details or instructions concerning the meeting, either in the body of a message or in the form of an attachment.

• Email preserves a record of the communication, both for you and the attendees.

- If there is anything sensitive or controversial about the nature of the meeting, sending an email message allows you to choose your words carefully, and not get drawn into awkward discussions or arguments.

Perhaps the only disadvantage of email is that, especially if the meeting is convened on short notice, you can never be sure that all invitees will have looked at their email messages in time to prepare for the meeting. If you are worried that one or more invitees might deliberately ignore the invitation, it is possible to send out an email message that prompts the user to return an automated acknowledgement of receipt. This isn't a text reply to the message written by the receiver, but merely an electronically generated "proof of delivery". If you don't receive this response from one or more invitees as the time of the meeting is drawing near, you will have the option of phoning those from whom there has been no response.

When meetings or conferences are being arranged and a person outside of the company will be invited to attend, you have the same two options. However, in the case of a more formal conference that is planned farther in advance there is also the option of issuing written invitations and sending them through the mail. For special occasions these may be professionally printed and sent out with reply cards similar to wedding invitations.

Whatever method is used to inform participants about a meeting or conference, your message must answer all the same "w" questions journalists are proverbially taught to answer in their news stories: who, what, when, where, and why. Invitees need to know enough about the subject of the meeting to understand why they should be attending. (Note that information about "when" should also answer the question "how long": both the start time and the expected completion time should be indicated so participants can plan accordingly). Beyond that, the amount of information divulged in the invitation depends on the situation and the wishes of your manager. Staff members who are subordinate don't need to be persuaded or coaxed into attending. They simply need to be politely informed that their attendance is expected. However, if you are trying to prompt outsiders to attend a conference voluntarily, you may need to provide a good reason for them to want to attend. Sometimes brochures are sent with invitations to formal conferences, providing more details on the event and the benefits of attending. Alternatively, the company may post information about the conference on its website and coax invitees to visit the website for more information.

If people will be attending the event from outside the company it may also be relevant to include information about parking, special arrangements for overnight accommodations, meals served during the event, or any other relevant logistical details.

Invitees to a meeting or conference, whether from within or outside of the organization, also need to be informed about anything they are expected to bring to the meeting. If the meeting involves departmental employees, they may be asked to bring reports, sales data, progress reports on projects underway, or other pertinent items.

In addition to having the correct content and accurate information, anything that you prepare and disseminate for a meeting must be written and formatted professionally.

Assisting with Multi-Media Presentations

Regardless of the purpose of the meeting, whether it is to make an announcement to employees, a training session of some kind, or an attempt to impress a prospective client, these days meeting organizers often look for ways to do more than just talk. Increasingly there is an interest in making an event more interesting with multi-media presentations. Highly sophisticated meetings or conferences may make use of professionally prepared films, either made specially for the occasion or obtained and shown because of their relevance to the topic under discussion. However, software is now widely available that allows office staff with only modest computer skills to create simple but effective multi-media presentations.

Most office computers are equipped with a basic operating system such as Windows, and a package of multi-purpose office software such as Microsoft Office or the Star Office7 Office Suite. These software packages are all very similar, and once you learn any one of them you can quickly and easily adapt to another. Each has separate but interrelated programs for performing basic office tasks such as word processing, creating spreadsheets, and creating presentations. It is the program for presentations that is most relevant to our current discussion. It is not our purpose to teach you the technical details of using any particular brand of presentations software. For now we want you to become aware of the general capabilities of this software and how it relates to an administrative assistant's duties in helping to organize and assist in meetings and conferences.

Presentations software allows you to create a simple "slide show" type presentation on an ordinary office PC. You don't actually use the old fashioned "slides" made from squares of film. Rather, you create a series of images on your computer, and then use the software to play the images to an audience. The images may contain

words, photos, and graphics such as charts and graphs. The software assists you directly in creating the text that will go on your slides, and with basic types of charts. However, you can also import scanned photos or portions of text from other sources. Because all of the different parts of an office software suite are interrelated, documents produced using the word processing package or spreadsheets created with the spreadsheet package can be incorporated into the slide show. Most basic presentations do not include an audio track. Generally, the person leading the discussion or giving the lecture will speak to the audience, explaining the slides as they appear.

A slide show can be created and then tested on a regular PC. However rarely would the leader of a meeting ask participants to gather around a small computer monitor to watch the presentation during the actual event.

Rather, there is special audiovisual equipment that is designed to interact with a PC in order to project the presentation in a larger format. Sometimes a big screen T.V. is used to display the presentation. More often, special projectors and screens are used. Companies that frequently hold meetings or training events where this type of material is used will often have dedicated conference rooms where the projection equipment is permanently installed. The screen may be permanently mounted onto a wall or may pull down only when needed. The data projector may be attached to the ceiling and angled at the screen.

In most cases data projectors are just a relay between a PC and a screen.

You still need to have some type of computer in the room on which the program is actually run. Some offices will keep a PC in the conference room for this purpose. The person giving the presentation will usually burn it to a CD or DVD after it has been created and tested. The CD can be loaded onto the conference room PC, and then the presentations program stored on the PC activates to present the show. In other cases, the person giving the talk will load the show onto a laptop computer, bring it into the conference room, and connect it to the data projector.

Slide shows can be timed to run automatically, with the interval between slides pre-set by the creator. However, in most cases the person giving the show will also have a remote control device, to pause the show, or speed up the progress from one slide to another.

In your job as an administrative assistant you may or may not have any direct involvement with the production of slide shows. That may be the responsibility of your manager, or any outside guest who has been invited to give a presentation at the meeting. However, you will likely have a key role in coordinating the equipment and orchestrating the event. It is essential that you become thoroughly familiar with any special audiovisual equipment that is used in your place of work, as well as with the software that is used to launch presentations and the control devices for operating the equipment. You should have specific and detailed discussions before hand with the person who is leading the presentation, including, if time allows, a rehearsal. It is important to know exactly what the leader wants you to do and when. If the person leading the discussion is not thoroughly familiar with the equipment you may be expected to give a demonstration and help ensure that there are no surprises once the presentation is underway.

Often the person leading the discussion will want some of the most important slides to be printed on paper and presented as handouts to the other participants and guests. People don't tend to absorb complex written details simply by seeing them pass by on a screen, so often it is advantageous to have a "take home" version. Printing slides from a presentation is a very simple procedure.

The handouts you produce don't necessarily have to be exact copies of the slides. Slides often use words sparingly and show them in large letters. A typical slide show will make use of pictures or charts with captions, headings, and often bulleted lists of key items that summarize the main points of the presentation. It is not practical to ask people to read large amounts of text

projected on a screen. However, when it comes to producing handouts based on the slides, the material can be copied into the word processing part of the software suite where it can be reformatted and expanded, if need be.

Preparing Minutes of a Meeting

The term "minutes" refers to a condensed report on what happened during a meeting, using a standardized format. The aim is to preserve a record and provide a brief summary for the benefit of participants who need to follow up on items that were discussed, or to inform others who did not attend the meeting but need to know what happened. The aim is to convey information clearly and concisely with a minimum of verbiage. The use of a standardized format or "template" helps in collecting and presenting the required information.

As an administrative assistant it may be your responsibility to prepare minutes of meetings for your manager. During the meeting itself you will need to take detailed notes so as to capture the information that will be needed for the minutes. Then the minutes are prepared using word processing software. Naturally, you will need to adapt the format to conform to the specific nature of the meeting as well as company policies and managerial preferences.

There is nothing particularly complicated about the note taking process. Obviously you need to be familiar with the style and content of previously prepared minutes so you will know what type of information you need to capture. It is vital to record the names of participants, as well as any specific dates, times, or data that may be relevant to the minutes.

It is important to know the names and affiliations (job titles and employers) of meeting participants. If you do not already know the people involved you should ask for the spellings of names and formal titles before the meeting gets started, as you are introduced to the participants. Sometimes participants will give you business cards that provide the key information. In other cases you may wish to circulate a sign-in sheet where the participants will write down their names, titles, and contact information (email and phone numbers). Make sure they understand your role in preparing the minutes so they will understand why you are collecting this information.

The general template or format for the minutes will likely be similar to the following:

Name of Corporation or Organization
Name of Department, Group or Committee

(Title of Meeting, if any)
Meeting time and location

Present:
(names and titles or affiliations of attendees)

Minutes
1. Name of first topic discussed
A brief summary in prose or point form of the main items discussed under this topic, including the key people who made various proposals or concerns. Depending on the complexity of the discussions this may take only a couple of lines, or several inches of text on the page, but rarely more than that.

2. Name of second topic discussed
(continued in this format until all topics are described)

The last topic may be the time, date, and place of the next scheduled meeting of the group.

Final (indicates the final, approved draft)
Name of administrative assistant/secretary and date

The specific nature of the minutes varies depending on the degree of formality of the meeting. In the case of a very formal meeting, such as a meeting of a Board of Directors, the minutes need to capture some other technicalities. The following are typical of additional elements that often apply in the case of a formal meeting:

• It may be necessary to ascertain and record that a "quorum" of participants are present. The term "quorum" refers to the minimum number of official participants, as stipulated in the group's charter or rules of operation, that must be present at certain types of meetings in order for any type of vote to take place at the meeting.

• At formal meetings the first order of business is often the reading and approval of the minutes from the previous meeting. Participants may already have been given copies of the minutes. However, since the minutes serve as a formal record of the meeting, the board must approve them. If there are any inaccuracies or omissions they must be corrected.

• Sometimes topics at a meeting are divided into "old business" and "new business" with the old business discussed first. Old business refers to any ongoing issues that have previously been discussed. Often a written "agenda" is prepared and distributed to participants prior to the start of a formal meeting. It lists the topics to be discussed in the order in which the group leader plans to raise them. Where time is of the essence the group leader may elect to establish an approximate length of time to discuss each topic, in order to cover all the topics in the time allotted for the meeting. If discussions on a particular topic cannot resolve the issue in approximately the amount of time allotted for it, the group leader may propose to carry the topic forward and discuss it again as "old business" at the start of the next scheduled meeting.

• Often the purpose of formal meetings is to receive approval for various proposals that are being brought forward to a group of decision makers. Decisions about such proposals, as well as decisions about various aspects of the meeting, may be put to a vote. Whenever a vote is taken it is important to record the outcome of the vote in numbers, for and against.

• Sometimes a vote will be initiated by a "motion". A motion is a formally worded proposal put to the group by a member. For example, a member of the group may request a motion for action to be taken by the group in response to information that has been presented. Before it is put to a vote, a motion must generally be "seconded". This means that another member of the group gives approval for bringing the motion to a vote. This is generally just a formal courtesy, although its purpose is to discourage frivolous votes that are of interest only to one party. When taking notes for minutes of a formal meeting you should record the names of the persons who make and second a motion unless instructed otherwise. Sometimes there are minor procedural details that require a motion, which must be seconded, though not a vote — such as a motion to adjourn the meeting.

In some cases you may be asked to bring a tape recorder to a meeting and make a recording of the entire event. If this is the case, make sure ahead of time that:

1. you know how to use the equipment

2. you know what type of microphone to use and where to place it in order to pick up the voices of all participants

3. you have an adequate supply of blank tapes on hand, know how long each lasts, and will be suitably positioned to change tapes if and when necessary.

You also need to know the company's policy and your manager's wishes with regard to labeling, storing, transcribing or eventually disposing of the tapes.

It should be pointed out that making a tape recording is not a substitute for taking accurate written notes during the meeting. Tapes do not record certain key information, such as who is speaking, and some passages may be garbled due to technical difficulties or an inarticulate speaker. Also, it will take you as long to listen to the tapes a second time as it took to record them, which is generally not an effective use of your time. At times you may wish to double check certain information by fast forwarding through the tapes until you find a key spot in the discussion. However, learn how to glean the main points from a discussion and convey them in a concise summary fashion. Rarely will anyone want you to produce a word-for-word transcript of everything that was said during the meeting, except under special circumstances.

Handling Meeting Logistics

As an administrative assistant you may also be responsible for looking after the practical, logistical aspects of a meeting that is being led by your manager. Meetings don't just happen. Besides sending out notices or invitations, and assisting with the preparation of materials to be used during the meeting, there are also basic physical or "logistical" details that need to be arranged. Depending on the nature of the meeting, you may be asked to arrange or assist with any or all of the following:

• Booking space for the meeting, if it will not take place in office space you control. This might involve a shared conference room somewhere in the company's facilities, or a rented space at a hotel or convention center. When booking a space ensure that the person accepting the booking knows how many people will be attending.

• Arranging for parking and informing participants of the arrangements that have been made.

• If the meeting will be held during winter in a northern climate, or where there is a risk of rain, and participants from outside the company will be attending provide a convenient and secure place to store coats, umbrellas, and boots.

• Assisting long distance attendees with booking accommodations at local hotels.

• Reserving any computer or audiovisual equipment that will be needed for the meeting, and ensuring that it is set up as needed in time for the event. It is a good idea whenever possible to visit the site ahead of time, if you are not already familiar with it. Plan a layout for the event, taking into account seating arrangements, natural lighting, and the location of outlets. You may need to ensure that you have extension cords of sufficient length. Extension cords should never extend across a path that large numbers of people will need to cross, and if there is a risk that anyone might trip over a cord it should be taped securely to the floor with duct tape at the likely point of crossing, and the potential tripping hazard should be mentioned.

• Ensure that the space will contain a suitable number of tables and chairs, and that they will be arranged according to your manager's wishes. For highly interactive or participatory discussions it is a good idea to seat the attendees so that everyone can see everyone else, perhaps in a square or circular arrangement depending on the size and shape of the room and the number of people who will be assembled there.

• If you are helping to arrange a large meeting or conference it may be necessary to have a sound system consisting of one or more microphones and speakers so that persons leading the discussion or giving presentations can be heard clearly. If you are holding the meeting at a hotel or conference center the facility may be able to provide you with the needed equipment and arrange to have it set up for you. In other cases you may need to rent this equipment and have it set up by a service company, or a technical department within your own organization. Be sure to confirm all arrangements and ensure that there is time to test the equipment, well before the actual start of the proceedings.

• You may need to provide for or arrange for refreshments and/or meals in the case of an extended meeting or conference. This may mean coffee makers and pastries or a full professionally catered lunch or dinner. Make arrangements for the necessary equipment or serving staff well in advance — don't assume they will be available on short notice. Be sure you know the company's policies and your manager's expectations with regard to any food or beverage service. There may be a particular caterer with whom the company has a standing contract. If you are using rented facilities, be sure that the owner of the facility approves your plan. Many hotels make ideal meeting and convention sites because they are able to provide items such as large coffee urns, as well as meals and servers from their own restaurant. If a meal will be served during the event attendees should be informed of this fact in advance. In the case of a half-day meeting, it is generally expected that there will be at least one "coffee break" midway through the event. Sometimes when an extended meeting involves only company staff members, rather than catering the event at the company's expense, a take-out order from a local restaurant will be ordered for lunch or a snack. Whenever a large number of people are involved it is wise to arrange for this in advance whenever possible. Many restaurants these days allow you to place orders by fax or email. Some restaurants are better than others at catering business luncheons or other affairs and, in consultation with your manager, you should choose one that has a reputation for delivering quality service.

• Apart from refreshments served during breaks or at lunchtime, you may be expected to arrange for clean glasses and pitchers of ice water to be available.

• For some meetings and conferences you may be asked to prepare nametags for the participants. Be sure to double-check the spelling of names.

• If possible, try to get to the meeting place well before invitees start to arrive. Besides ensuring that all of the furniture and equipment is as it should be, ensure that the light, heat, or air conditioning is at a comfortable level.

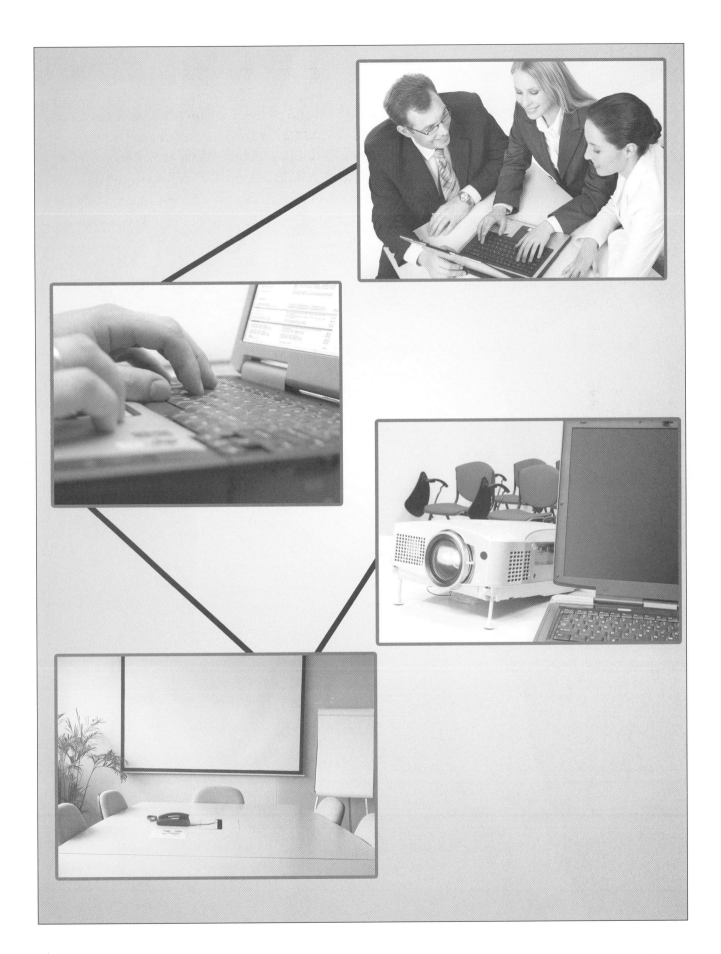

Chapter 4

MAKING
Travel Arrangements

The Nature of Business Travel

Business travel isn't as popular an activity today as it was a couple of decades ago. There are a couple of reasons for this. First of all globalization and increased foreign competition have caused

many North American corporations to become "leaner and meaner". Expenses are carefully watched and rationalized. If a trip isn't really necessary, other means of communicating or accomplishing the long distance interaction are being selected. Increased fuel costs have added to the cost of travel, and international terrorism has led to heightened tension and security, especially on international flights.

Nonetheless, some degree of business travel is still inevitable, and helping to make travel arrangements remains an important part of an administrative assistant's duties in many organizations. In this section of the text we will profile the basic duties associated with making travel arrangements. Naturally, you will be expected to follow the preferences and policies of your employer in any specific job situation.

Travel arrangements can be broadly divided into the following categories:

1) Booking transportation, which usually means airline tickets, though occasionally one might travel by train, depending on the distance involved and the urgency of reaching the destination quickly.

2) Booking ground transportation and transfers. This could include renting a car at the destination, or other means of getting around, such as limousines, airport buses, or local public transportation.

3) Booking hotel accommodations.

We can conclude the typical travel-related duties of the administrative assistant by adding the following two items to the list:

4) Helping to arrange financial resources for the trip, which may involve requisitioning a check for a travel advance, the purchase of traveler's checks, or arranging for a payment on a company credit card so as to open up a greater disposable credit balance in the account.

5) Assisting the manager with completing financial documentation and/or reports on business activities after the trip. Most employers use special forms to report travel expenses, breaking them down into categories. Receipts must usually be submitted to substantiate the expenditures.

The role of the administrative assistant in any or all of these activities is influenced by the companies organizational structure and policies for booking travel arrangements. Some large companies have special staff who make arrangements on behalf of executives. Others have a standing contract with a local travel agency to take care of most of these functions, and the role of the administrative assistant is merely to liaise with the agency to communicate the pertinent dates and details of a specific trip. The travel agent will then make the reservations, secure the tickets, and produce a printed itinerary — which shows all of the flights and ground transfers in consecutive order, together with times, flight numbers and pertinent details.

If the company doesn't make use of a travel agent (which is relatively rare these days, since agencies often receive commissions from the airlines and other service providers, so there is little or no cost to the company in using the services of the agency), then the administrative assistant may need to phone the airlines and hotels, or make online arrangements via their websites. A major advantage of working with a travel agent is that, in addition to saving the company's staff time and hassles having to make all the

arrangements independently, good travel agents have a thorough understanding of fare structures and options for places to stay, and can therefore secure more advantageous bookings for their clients. If you are ever asked to assume these duties by yourself, you need to research the destinations and the carrier options carefully and thoroughly to make sure you know what is available and comparative cost factors before making any choices. In this section we will assume that the administrative assistant is interacting with a travel agent, since this is the most common scenario.

Air Travel Arrangements

One important reason many companies have cut back on business travel is that for a long time airlines have "preyed" on the business traveler as their main source of profitability. Many airfares are structured to place the business traveler at a disadvantage and force them to pay a higher fare than might be available to personal travelers. You will find that many of the discounted rates require booking well ahead of time (something a business traveler is not always able to do, as business situations evolve and change rapidly) or force the traveler to stay over a Saturday (which business travelers don't often wish to do, since their business will likely be concluded Friday and the extra night will increase costs for accommodations and meals). When you don't have that kind of flexibility in planning your stay at a destination, you are sometimes forced to pay full fares — although some airlines are now offering business travelers much more attractive rates without so many restrictions.

To compensate for charging higher fares to business travelers, many airlines have tried to maintain their business by offering a higher level of in-flight service. Traditionally there were three classes of service on most larger flights: first class, business class, and coach. First class was by far the most expensive and only appealed to wealthy people or business executives. Business class was an attempt by airlines to pamper business travelers a bit more than the "regular passengers" in coach without quite the level of luxury offered in the first class cabin at the front of the plane. We are using the past tense because, while some airlines still maintain this class system, there are an increasing number of "no frills" airlines that have done away with this approach, offering all passengers the same fares and the same level of service. As companies begin to scrutinize business expenses more carefully, increasingly their employees are being asked to travel on these newer, cheaper airlines whenever possible.

Regardless of the airline or the class of service, there are some basic terms related to types of airline flights with which you should be familiar.

Nonstop flight — As the name implies, this is any flight that goes from the point of departure to the destination without landing at any other point along the way. Not only is this the quickest way to travel from point A to point B, but it is generally the most reliable. The more often a traveler needs to stop along the way or change planes, the greater the risk of problems or delays due to bad weather or some other unplanned difficulty.

Direct flight — This term means that a traveler can go from point A to point B without having to change planes, but the plane makes one or more additional stops before reaching the final destination. The extra stops increase the length of the flight significantly. However, they save the traveler from the potential hassles and risk factors associated with having to make "connecting flights".

Connecting flight — This term applies in cases where in order to reach a final destination, a traveler needs to stop at one or more cities along the way, get off the plane and change to another plane that operates as a completely separate flight and flight number. There are two main types of connecting flights, those made with the same airline and those made with a different airline. Besides the delays and hassles associated with having to make one's way across a busy airport, sometimes to a separate terminal building, the main risk associated with connecting flights is that if the first flight is delayed for some reason, the traveler may miss the connecting flight. This can cause serious problems if the airline is not able to get the traveler booked onto another flight that same day. While this is always a serious hassle, connecting flights with the same airline are usually a bit safer in the sense that the airlines tend to feel a greater obligation to passengers who are continuing their travel with them. If they cannot find a connecting flight that day, they may pay to have the passenger spend the night in a hotel until a flight is available. Sometimes when the connecting flight is with a different airline, neither airline seems to feel the same duty to the traveler.

Shuttle flight — Some airlines operate so many flights between two nearby cities or between one airport and another that it is not necessary to have a reservation to get on the flight. The flights may leave frequently and accommodation is on a first come, first served basis.

Sometimes there are limited options for traveling from one destination to another, either in general, or in terms of bookings that are available on a particular day. All else being equal in terms of fares and service, the administrative assistant should generally select the fastest and most secure flight arrangement. In general this means that non-stops are better than directs, directs are better than connecting flights, and connecting flights with the same carrier are better than those where it is necessary to switch carriers. However, if you have no choice but to select a less desirable option, layover time and time of day are also factors to be considered. Layover refers to the waiting time between flights. While a long layover is generally undesirable because it wastes time and delays arrival at the destination, layovers that are too short increase the risk that the traveler will miss the connecting flight. Before accepting any booking that involves a layover of less than two hours, consider and inquire about the following:

1) How far will the traveler have to go to get from one flight to the other? In some cases it may be just a few gates down within the same terminal. In other cases it might mean traveling to a terminal that is so far from the point of arrival that a shuttle bus is necessary. Transfers from one terminal to another can be a big problem when one has to make a tight connection, especially these days with increased security screening at airports. When you transfer from one plane to another within the same airline, often it's simply a case of walking a few gates farther along the same corridor and you don't have to pass through airport security again. However, this is not the case if you have to move from one wing to another within the same terminal, or particularly if you have to leave the airport building and travel to a separate terminal building to catch the next flight. Sometimes the shuttle between buildings is nothing compared to the delay of having to wait in line to be screened all over again, especially during peak travel times when the terminal is really busy.

2) What is the on-time record of the airport where the change of flights will be made? Some major airports are so busy that they frequently operate behind schedule.

3) Are seasonal weather factors apt to come into play? In some areas of the country bad weather can be anticipated more often at certain times of the year and additional layover time may be needed.

4) At what time of day will the transfer take place? Most airports are at their busiest at the same time most freeways are: first thing in the morning and the supper hour. Flights are more likely to be delayed at these times. However, one advantage of traveling earlier in the day is that if a connecting flight is missed there are more options available for reaching the destination that day. An evening connection is risky, especially if the layover is short, because if the connecting flight is missed the traveler may be stranded at the stopover point until the following day.

Additional general information you should know about booking and purchasing airline tickets is:

• These days it is possible and often desirable to consult airline timetables and order tickets online. Be aware, though, that airline timetables and fare codes are a complex and often confusing business. This is why many business people leave it to a professional travel agent, who is usually in a better position to sort out the best deals. Naturally, you can phone the airline directly and get a ticketing agent to help you. However, you cannot always presume that these agents will inform you of the best options, especially if the best option is with another carrier!

Whenever you book a flight at anything less than the full fare, you should be aware of any restrictions that apply. Common restrictions include any or all of the following:

• minimum interval at which special bookings can be made prior to the flight date

• minimum length of stay

• minimum length of time by which the ticket must be purchased after it is booked

• penalty for making any changes to the reservations

• nonrefundable tickets, or a severe financial penalty for any changes or refunds

• option to purchase insurance that will reduce or eliminate the penalties if reservations are changed or canceled due to confirmed illness

You should also be aware of some terms related to specific types of tickets and itineraries.

One-way ticket. As the name implies, you are purchasing a ticket to go from point A to point B. This doesn't mean you won't eventually return to point A, but you are not committing to doing so with the air carrier in question. Although some newer airlines are making exceptions, airlines usually charge higher fares for one-way tickets and do not offer special discounts or seat sales.

Round-trip ticket. This is the classic airline booking where flights both to and from the destination are booked and paid for as part of the same ticket purchase. Note that a true round trip ticket specifies the dates and flight numbers for the entire trip. Most special fare offers are applicable mainly or exclusively for purchase of round trip tickets.

Open ticket. This is a ticket for which the return trip is paid for at the time of purchase, but a return date is not specified. The ticket holder will need to contact the airline and make a reservation for a return flight, and the airline will honor the ticket on any flight that isn't fully booked. As with one-way tickets, many airlines don't offer attractive fares on open tickets, and it should be noted that most airlines allow you to change your reservations on full fare tickets anyway. So, if a holder of a full fare ticket is not able to make the flight and needs to take a later one, the change can be made, often without penalty, by notifying the airline.

Open-leg ticket. This type of ticket is issued when a person will make part of a journey by some method other than air travel. For example, a person may fly to one city, then drive to a second city and eventually fly home from that city. The trip by car between the two cities is the open leg.

Standby ticket. This is somewhat like an open ticket except there is no confirmed flight number in either direction. The ticket holder may sometimes obtain a lower fare by agreeing to fly at the airline's convenience rather than with a firm reservation. This means that you are listed as a standby passenger for a flight and must wait until the final minutes to see if a seat is available. If not, you have to list as standby on the next available flight and try again. This isn't quite as foolish as it may sound, since there are almost always a few no-shows for any flight. However, a business traveler would rarely make this sort of uncertain arrangement, and many airlines no longer offer standby

tickets at a special fare. However, a person who holds a full fare ticket or an open ticket may wish to be listed as a standby passenger on a flight that is sold out, hoping that they can get a seat and thereby fly sooner than the first confirmed reservation presently offered to them.

Car Rentals

Car rentals can be booked directly by contacting the rental company or through a travel agent. Large car rental companies often have outlets at several locations in major cities, including the airport. Picking up a car at the airport is generally most convenient for business travelers. Many rental agencies offer options for "accelerated" pick-up and drop-off service. If proper arrangements have been made, the renter can proceed immediately to the car lot and not have to stand in line at a counter in the airport terminal.

Rental costs vary depending on the type of car selected and the length and time of the rental. Weekday rentals are generally more expensive than weekend packages. When cars are rented or leased for an extended period, the daily rate can be significantly less. Rental plans vary depending on how much of the fee is built into the basic daily rate and how much is charged through extra fees such as mileage. The desirability of

one plan or another depends on how much use the renter plans to make of the vehicle. If the vehicle will only be used for short trips around town between business sites and accommodations, it is generally best to pick the lowest available daily rate. It will include a specified base number of miles, then a per mile charge thereafter. If the renter plans to drive for long distances or intervals, a more all-inclusive price is better, even if it means that the base rate is higher.

Car rental agencies offer options for insurance coverage. You can pay extra for a more complete insurance coverage, or pay less for only minimal coverage. Before making a booking it is important to check with your manager regarding company policies and personal preferences for insurance, type of vehicle, and rental plan options.

If the renter will be traveling some distance with the vehicle, it is important to inquire into the rental company's policies and options for vehicle return. Some rental outlets expect you to return the vehicle to the same outlet where you picked it up. Others will allow the vehicle to be returned to any outlet in the same city. Others will allow you to drive the vehicle out of the state or province and return it at the point of destination, but they may charge a fee for costs to return the vehicle to the original outlet. The point is, never make assumptions when booking any sort of transportation arrangements. Explain the needs thoroughly to the reservationist or travel agent and make sure that the arrangement booked is fully suitable and practical for the traveler's needs. Always double-check any tickets or printed reservation records that you receive to insure that they conform with your original instructions and expectations.

Hotel Reservations

Hotel reservations can be made by contacting the hotel directly, or through a travel agent. Rates vary significantly depending on the class of the hotel and the length of stay. Many frequent-business travelers obtain special corporate rates, but in order to take advantage of this option an arrangement must be set up by the company with the hotel in advance. In addition to obtaining special rates, corporate guests can often obtain billing privileges, meaning that a bill for the stay will be sent to the company and does not have to be paid by the guest at the time of checkout.

With the exception of pre-arranged corporate accounts, most hotels expect to be paid at the time service is rendered. In addition, they generally expect a credit card number in order to guarantee a reservation. This means that unless the reservation is cancelled within the stipulated time frame the credit card will be charged. You should be aware of the hotel's polices in this regard. Some hotels will hold a room for a certain time without a guaranteed reservation, but a credit card guarantee is needed in order to hold a room for a late arrival. Thus, the time your business traveler will be arriving at the hotel may be a factor in the type of reservation you need to make.

Another factor in choosing a hotel and/or the level of accommodations and service is what the traveler plans to do while staying at the hotel. The standard hotel offers a room with a private bathroom. A hotel restaurant serves meals and offers room service. There may be a mini-bar in the room that allows for self-serve refreshments and snacks, for a fee. This type of accommodation tends to suit the business traveler who uses the hotel room as a place to relax, eat, and sleep after a day spent conducting business activities at other nearby locations. However, there is another option. Sometimes the traveler needs to conduct business meetings at the hotel, rather than at some other office site in town. In such cases it is possible to select accommodations that provide the guest with more than a bedroom. Hotel "suites" also include a separate sitting room that can be set up for a small meeting. Some also include private

kitchen facilities, which may appeal to guests who are away on extended assignments.

Hotels that cater to business travelers also offer other services to assist the guest in conducting business while staying at the facility. These may include internet access, fax machines and message services, as well as the option to rent equipment or separate conference rooms for business presentations. Before booking a hotel stay for a business traveler, it is a good idea to inquire about business services and options that may be available at the establishment.

Travel Documents

International travelers need special documents. As an administrative assistant it will not likely be your responsibility to obtain these documents for your manager, but you should be aware of them.

The primary travel document is the passport. Passports are issued by the country of which the traveler is a citizen. They include a photo, a signature, and biographical data used in identification. There is a fee for obtaining a passport, and generally a delay period in processing a passport application, so it cannot be obtained at the last minute. Once issued, passports are good for several years, but they expire at a specified date and need to be renewed.

At one time passports were not required to travel from one country to another within North America and parts of the Caribbean. However, since the events of September 11, 2001 international security has tightened, and now passports are recommended or required for all international travel.

A visa is an additional document or authorization, that is needed to travel to many foreign countries. In general, a North American traveler can travel freely through North America, Europe, and other places without any special visa, showing only the standard passport. Visas are issued by foreign countries specifically to grant entry into their countries. They are issued for a specific trip and purpose within specified dates. Visas need to be obtained from consular officials of the country in question well in advance of intended travel. Many visas are stamped directly onto passports in the back pages of the passport booklet.

Some countries also require International Certificates of Vaccination as proof that a traveler has been vaccinated against serious diseases that may be indigenous to the area. These forms can generally be obtained through the local department of health and signed by the physician who administers the vaccination. Whether or not vaccinations are required, they are highly recommended for travel to any tropical or Third World country.

Preparing Travel Itineraries

You may be asked to assist your manager by preparing a travel itinerary. There are two basic types of itineraries. The first type shows only travel and accommodation arrangements. If you obtain reservations through a travel agent, the agency will provide this type of itinerary. It shows flight numbers, departure and arrival times, any pre-booked ground transportation, and hotel accommodations. It generally includes booking or reservations numbers.

The second type of itinerary may include the above information, but it also provides a list of scheduled appointments and events during the trip. When the traveler is attending a seminar or conference, the detailed schedule may be provided in advance by the organizers. If the traveler will be attending privately arranged meetings and events, then the itinerary will include a listing similar to a daily appointment schedule that would be kept for in-office meetings.

All itineraries should be clear and concise, using a standard format and as little verbiage as possible. An itinerary is simply a memory-refresher and a way to record significant information. Itineraries are always presented in chronological order by day and time, and often look much like pages from a standard day planner.

It is important to produce at least two printed copies of an itinerary, one for your manager and one for yourself, so you can follow your boss's activities from the office and be aware of what is taking place and when. Today most people also like to store itineraries on office PCs and laptops. In this way if changes are made they can be entered onto the existing template, and copies of the revised schedule can be emailed to any other party who should be made aware of the changes.